THE
PUB JOKE

BOOK 3
Ever!

This is a Carlton Book

This edition published by Carlton Books Limited 1999

ISBN 1 85868 830 2

Printed and bound in Great Britain

THE BEST PUB JOKE

BOOK 3 Ever!

DAVID SOUTHWELL
WITH SAM WIGAND

CARLTON

Contents

Dogs & Ducks	7
The After-Work Crowd	41
Doctor's Orders	77
Guys & Dolls	121
The Great White Telephone to God	159
Assorted Crisps & Snacks	181
Around the Pub	225
You're Not From Round 'Ere, Are You?	263
Theme Nights	293

Dogs & Ducks

1

Jokes about the Animal Kingdom

You're nobody until you've been ignored by a cat!

****

How can you tell if you're in an elevator with an elephant? You can smell the peanuts on his breath.

****

It's always blackest just before you step on the cat.

****

If you're colour-blind, how do you tell a grape from an elephant? Stamp on it a while. If you don't get any wine, it's an elephant.

****

What do you know when you see three elephants walking down the street wearing pink sweatshirts? They're all on the same team.

****

How do you know if you pass an elephant? You can't get the toilet seat down.

How do you catch a yellow elephant? First find a yellow elephant. Then look at it through the wrong end of a telescope, pick it up with a pair of tweezers and put it in a matchbox.

****

Make your mark in the world, or at least spray in each corner.

****

Why do elephants have trunks? Where else would they pack their luggage?

****

From an Associated Press bulletin: When a San Francisco insecticide manufacturer ran a contest in August, 1994, looking for the most cockroach-infested house in the country to demonstrate its pest control prowess, Rosemary Mitchell of Tulsa, Oklahoma, really wanted to win, and she did. The prize: a house call from a roach expert, entomologist Austin Frishman, aka television's 'Dr Cockroach', who began work on the home after estimating that her one-story house harboured between 60,000 and 100,000 roaches. Mitchell said, "I keep a pretty clean house," but admitted that she had to check the bed thoroughly every night and shake the shower curtains off every morning. Frishman said that he has seen a lot worse and rated Mitchell's house only a "three" on a scale of one to five.

****

Why is it that elephants never forget? Well, what do they have to remember?

****

In ancient Rome, the cat was considered a symbol of liberty. Anyone who watches a cat can see that he always does exactly as he pleases.

****

Have you heard of the wallet made of elephant foreskin? When you rub it, it turns into a briefcase.

****

The other day, I was walking my dog around my building...on the ledge. Some people are afraid of heights. Not me, I'm afraid of widths.

****

A man and his dog walk into a bar. The man says: "I'll bet you a round of drinks that my dog can talk." Bartender: "Yeah! Sure...go ahead." Man asks the dog: "What covers a house?" Dog says: "Roof!" Man asks the dog: "How does sandpaper feel?" Dog says: "Rough!" Man asks the dog: "Who was the greatest Baseball player of all time?" Dog says: "Ruth!" Man says to the bartender: "Pay up. I told you he could talk." Bartender throws both of them out the door. Sitting on the sidewalk, the dog looks at the man and says: "Should I have said Gehrig, then?"

****

What do elephants use for vibrators? Epileptic pigmies.

****

Cats are intended to teach us that not everything in nature has a function.

****

A snail got mugged by two tortoises. When he went to the police, they questioned him as to what happened. He said: "I don't know; it all happened so quickly!"

****

What do elephants use for tampons? Sheep.

****

How do porcupines make love? Veerry carefully!

****

Why do elephants have long trunks? Because sheep don't have strings.

****

What has two tails, two trunks and five feet? An elephant with spare parts.

****

What did the peanut say to the elephant? Nothing, peanuts can't talk.

****

What did the vet say to the dog who kept licking his balls? "Thanks darling."

****

Three agricultural scientists were determined to discover how much a pig could eat before it just had to take a shit. To this end they procured a Yorkshire sow and pushed a large cork into her arse. After six weeks of force feeding, the sow was the size of the Goodyear airship and threatening to burst. Being humane types, the scientists agreed that the cork must now be removed. No-one wished to volunteer for the job, however, so in true scientific tradition, they decided to train a monkey for the task and swiftly put a small gibbon through a crash course in cork-pulling. The day came and the pig was air-lifted out to the desert for safety's sake. Special equipment was set up to monitor the event. Picture the scene: In the middle of the desert, the pig. Behind the pig, the monkey. One mile behind him, the first scientist with a video camera. One mile behind that scientist are the other two scientists with a seismometer. Finally, the monkey reaches up and pulls out the cork. SPLAT! When the massive geyser has subsided, the two scientists find themselves knee-deep in pigshit. Grabbing shovels they wade forward and dig out the first man who has been buried up to his neck. When they free him they find that he is laughing hysterically. "What's so funny?" they ask. "You should have seen the monkey trying to get the cork back in!"

****

The more people I meet, the more I like my dog.

****

Why do elephants prefer peanuts to caviar? Peanuts are easier to get at the pub.

****

Why do hummingbirds hum? Because they don't know the words.

****

How do you know if there's an elephant in bed with you? She has a big 'E' on her pyjama jacket pocket.

****

How do you know if there is an elephant under the bed? Your nose is touching the ceiling.

****

How can you tell if an elephant has been in your refrigerator? Footprints in the butter.

****

How do you know if there are two elephants in your fridge? Two sets of footprints in the butter.

How do you know if there are three elephants in your fridge? Can't get the fridge door closed.

****

How do you know if there are four elephants in your fridge? There's a Mini parked outside it.

****

Why are there so many elephants running around free in the jungle? The fridge isn't large enough to hold them all.

****

How do you put an elephant into a fridge? Open the Mini door, take the elephant out, open the fridge, put the elephant inside, close the fridge.

****

The Lion, King of Beasts, gathered all the animals for a meeting. All of them showed up except the elephants. Why? They were stuck in the Mini.

****

Why did the turtle cross the road? To get to the Shell garage.

****

Why did the pervert cross the road? His dick was stuck in the chicken.

****

I went to the cinema the other day and in the front row was an old man and with him was his dog. It was a sad, funny kind of film, you know the type. In the sad part, the dog cried his eyes out, and in the funny part, the dog laughed its head off. This happened all the way through the film. After the film had ended, I decided to go and speak to the man. "That's the most amazing thing I've seen," I said. "That dog really seemed to enjoy the film. It's remarkable!" "Yeah, it is," said the man. "He hated the book."

****

An elephant is walking through the jungle when she gets a thorn in her foot. She is in absolute agony when she sees an ant strolling by. The elephant asks the ant for help but the ant refuses, unless the elephants is prepared to let the ant have his wicked way with her. "Anything! Anything!" replies the elephant. So, out comes the thorn and up gets the ant and proceeds to enjoy himself. Meanwhile, in a tree directly above them, a monkey, who witnessed the whole episode, was in fits of laughter. He laughed so much he fell out of the tree on top of the elephant. “Ouch!”, says the elephant. “Yeah,” says the ant, “take some more, bitch!”

****

Why do elephants wear pink tennis shoes? White ones get dirty too fast.

****

When you go out into the world, always remember, being placed on a pedestal is a right, not a privilege.

****

The Cat agenda: variety is the spice of life. One day, ignore people; the next day, annoy them. Only play with them when they’re busy.

****

Three rats are sitting at the bar talking. The first says: “I’m so hard, once I ate a whole bag full of rat poison!” The second says, “Well I’m well hard, once I was caught in a rat trap and I gnawed it apart!” Then the third rat gets up and says, “‘Bye chaps, I’m off home to screw the cat...”

The life sentence of Taro the dog was commuted in February 1994, permitting his release from the Bergen County Jail and his deportation from New Jersey. Taro had been sentenced to die under the state's "vicious dog" law, but appeals had continued until Taro had spent more than 1,000 days behind bars in his climate-controlled kennel and had cost American taxpayers more than $100,000 in expenses.

****

So this mouse walks in the jungle with his elephant friend, looks back and says: "Wow, look how much dust we leave behind!"

****

Why do seagulls live near the sea? Because if they lived near the bay, they would be called bagels.

****

A butcher is leaning on the counter towards the close of day when a wee dog wi' a basket in its jaws comes pushin' through the door. "An' wot's this then?" he asks. The dog knocks the basket sharply into the butcher's shins. "You li'tle bugger." As he reaches down to smack the dog, he notices a note and a tenner in the basket. The scribble on the note asks for three pounds of his best mince. The butcher reckons this is too easy. He goes to the window and reaches for the dried up stuff that's been sitting out all day. The dog growls at him. The butcher turns around and, glaring at the mut, gets the best mince from the fridge. Weighing out about 2 1/2 pounds, he drops in on the scale with his thumb. "Hmmmmm, a bit shy. Who'll know?" Again, the dog growls menacingly. "Alright, alright," as he throws on a generous half pound. He wraps it up, drops it in the basket, and drops in change from a fiver. The dog threatens to chew him off at the ankles. Another fiver goes in the basket. The butcher is quite impressed and decides to follow the little dog home. The dog quickly enters a high-rise building, pushes the lift button, enters the lift, and then pushes the button for the twelfth floor. The dog walks down the corridor and smartly bangs the basket on the door. The door opens, the dog's owner screams abuse at the dog and then tries to kick the dog inside. "Hey, what are you doing? That's a really smart dog you've got there." "Stoopid dog – that's the third time this week he's forgotten his key.

****

A dog went into a telegram office, took out a blank form and wrote, "Woof.. woof.. woof.. woof.. woof.. woof.. woof.. woof.. woof." The clerk examined the paper and told the dog: "There are only nine words here," he said. "You could send another 'woof' for the same price." "But," the dog replied, "that would be silly."

****

'If you pick up a starving dog and make him prosperous, he will not bite you. This is the principal difference between a dog and a man.' – Mark Twain

****

I turned on my lawn sprinkler as my dog was crossing the yard. He thought it was the lamp-post getting even with him.

****

Why do elephants paint the soles of their feet yellow? So that they can hide upside-down in custard.

****

Why do elephants wear sandals? So that they don't sink in the sand.

****

Why do sheep-shaggers wear green wellies? So they can stick the sheep's back legs down them.

****

How do you keep a skunk from smelling? Hold his nose.

Why do ostriches stick their heads in the ground? To look for the elephants who forgot to wear their sandals.

****

Psychiatrist: "What's wrong with your brother?" Sister: "He thinks that he's a chicken." Psychiatrist: "I see. And how long has be been acting like a chicken?" Sister: "Three years. We would have come in sooner, but we needed the eggs."

****

The Washington Post reported in September 1993 that at the Third Annual Fairfax County, Va. Slugfest, "Slippery" beat 49 other slugs in the Tour de Slug race. Also featured at the festival: slug face-painting, the slime toss, and the official drink – green "slimeade." A 12-year-old boy demonstrated his skill at flicking his tongue in and out of his mouth with his slug, Mickey, attached. He said that despite washing Mickey several times with soap beforehand, "the slime still sticks between your teeth. I've still got some slime from yesterday."

****

What did the one crocodile say to the other crocodile? What's with the long face?

Do you know why elephants paints their toenails red? So that no-one will see them hiding in the cherry trees. If you have never seen an elephant in a cherry tree, then you already know how effective it is.

****

Why don't they play poker on the African Savannah? There are too many cheetahs.

****

Why do elephants wear springs on their feet? So they can jump up in trees and rape monkeys.

****

A parrot has a habit of shagging chickens, so the farmer tells him that if he does it again he will pull out every feather on its head. The parrot jumps on the hens again, and his head feathers are duly pulled out. Meanwhile, the farmer's wife, who has pretensions to culture, is having a formal dinner. She appoints the parrot to be butler and to tell the guests where to put their hats and coats. The party proceeds without mishap, with the parrot announcing, "Ladies to the right! Gentlemen to the left!" Suddenly, two bald-headed men enter, and the parrot says: "You two chicken-fuckers come out to the hen house with me."

In a two-day period in New York City recently, a homeless man, a train maintenance worker, and a dog were killed on the subway tracks. Ninety people telephoned the Transit Authority to express concern about the dog, but only three called about the worker, and no-one phoned in about the homeless man.

****

Which pine has the longest needles? A porcupine.

****

I put contact lenses in my dog's eyes. They had little pictures of cats on them. Then I took one out and he ran around in circles.

****

Why do elephants not drink martinis? Have you ever tried getting an olive out of YOUR nose?

****

Two boy silkworms pursued a luscious girl silkworm. They ended up in a tie.

****

When do giraffes have eight legs? When there are two of them.

****

How do you train King Kong? Hit him with a rolled up newspaper-building.

****

Why do elephants have wrinkled knees? From playing marbles.

****

The Chicago Tribune reported in June 1994 on a local sex therapist, Robert Herd, who works exclusively helping animals to mate. He says a surprising number of dogs and horses exhibit sexual dysfunction.

****

A burglar has just made it into the house he's intending to ransack, and he's looking around for stuff to steal. All of a sudden, a little voice pipes up, "I can see you, and so can Jesus!" Startled, the burglar looks around the room. No one there at all, so he goes back to his business. "I can see you, and so can Jesus!" The burglar jumps again, and takes a longer look around the room. Over in the corner by the window, almost obscured by curtains, is a cage in which sits a budgie, who pipes up again: "I can see you, and so can Jesus!" "So what," says the burglar, "you're only a budgie!" To which the budgie replies: "Maybe, but 'Jesus' is the rottweiler!"

****

What is the loudest noise in the jungle? A giraffe eating cherries.

****

A panda spent the night in bed with a prostitute. The following morning as he is about ready to leave, the prostitute yells after him: "Hey, aren't you going to pay me?" The panda appears confused so she throws a dictionary at him and tells him to look up "prostitute". The definition reads: "A woman who engages in promiscuous sexual activity for pay." The panda throws the dictionary back at the prostitute and tells her to look up "panda". The definition reads: "An animal that eats bamboo, shoots, and leaves."

****

Two vampire bats wake up in the middle of the night, thirsty for blood. One says: "Let's fly out of the cave and get some blood." "We're new here," says the second one. "It's dark out, and we don't know where to look. We'd better wait until the other bats go with us." The first bat replies: "Who needs them? I can find some blood somewhere." He flies out of the cave. When he returns, he is covered with blood. The second bat says excitedly: "Where did you get the blood?" The first bat takes his friend to the mouth of the cave. Pointing into the night, he asks: "See that black building over there?" "Yes," the other bat answers. "Well," says the first bat, "I didn't."

****

Psychiatrist: "What's your problem?" Patient: "I think that I'm a chicken." Psychiatrist: "And how long has this been going on?" Patient: "Ever since I was an egg."

****

Why do hens lay eggs? If they dropped them, they'd break.

****

One hunter goes hunting and he tracks an elephant. He almost shoots it, then he looks into the elephant's eyes and decides that he is not up to it. Ten years later, he goes to the circus. There is a group of elephants performing. One of the elephants walks up to him and kicks him! Why?

****

Diner: "Do you serve chicken here?" Waiter: "We serve anyone sir."

****

What did Tarzan say when he saw 1,000 elephants coming over the hill? "Look, there's 1,000 elephants coming over the hill."

****

What did Tarzan say when he saw 1,000 elephants with sunglasses on, coming over the hill? Nothing, he didn't recognise them.

****

What's six feet long and hangs from trees in Africa? Elephant snot.

****

A farmer down the road has a fairly large herd of cows and three bulls. Each bull keeps a strict eye on his portion of the cows. A rumour comes around that the farmer is going to get another bull and the three bulls are standing in the field discussing this. The first bull says, "Well, there's no way he's going to get any of my cows." The second bull agrees, "Yeah, I'm not giving up any. He can wait till next year and get some of the new ones." The third bull who was a bit smaller says, "I don't have as many as you guys so I'm not giving any up." Finally, the new bull arrives. The first three gather at the edge of the field to watch him being unloaded from the trailer. To their consternation, the biggest, meanest Aberdeen Angus bull they have ever seen, with hooves like flint anvils, comes strolling down the ramp and glares at them. He's at least three times bigger than any of them. The first bull looks around nervously and says, "Well now, I suppose it would be a neighbourly thing to give this guy some cows. I think I'll give him twenty of mine." The second bull says, "Yeah, I guess so, I'll give him thirty of mine." They look over at the small bull. He's busy pawing the grass, snorting, and shaking his head. They go over and ask him what he's doing and suggest that he should give up some cows too. "Yes I know," he says, "I'm just making sure he knows I'm a bull!"

****

A blind man with a guide dog at his side walks into a department store. The man walks to the middle of the shop, picks up the dog by the tail and starts swinging it around in circles over his head. The manager, who has seen all this, thinks it a little odd, so, he approaches the blind man and says: "Pardon me. May I help you with something?" The blind man says: "No thanks, I'm just looking around."

****

Why do elephants wear tiny green hats? To sneak across a pool table without being seen.

****

One afternoon, there was a good witch who was flying along, when all of a sudden, she heard this soft crying from down below. When she landed, she saw a yellow frog. Touched by his sadness, the witch asked why he was crying. “Sniff. None of the other frogs will let me join in all their frog games. Boo hoo.” “Don’t cry, little one,” replied the witch, and with a wave of her magic wand, the frog turned green. All happy now, the frog was checking himself over when he noticed that his penis was still yellow. He asked an embarrassed witch about this, and she told him that there were some things that she just couldn’t do, but that the wizard could fix things up for him. So happily, the little green frog hippity-hopped along his merry way. Feeling quite happy about herself, the witch once more took to the skies, and once again, she heard some crying, but this time of a thunderous sort. So down to the ground she flew only to discover a pink elephant. The witch asked him why he was crying. “Sniff. None of the other elephants will let me join in all their elephant games. Boo hoo.” Now if you have ever seen an elephant cry, you know it to be a pathetic looking sight, but a pink elephant crying is just downright heart-breaking, and that is just how the witch felt. So once again, she waved her magic wand, and – poof – the elephant was all grey. All happy now, the elephant was checking himself all over when he noticed that his penis was still pink. He asked an embarrassed witch about this, and she told him that there were some things that she just couldn't do, but that the wizard would fix things up for him. At this point, the elephant started wailing again: "I don't know where the wizard is," he sobbed. "Oh that's easy," said the witch, "Just follow the yellow pricked toad."

****

What's the last thing that goes through a bee's mind when it hits a car windscreen at 70mph? Its arse.

****

What is worse than a giraffe with a sore throat? A centipede with athlete's foot.

****

Why didn't they invite the giraffe to the party? He was a pain in the neck to talk to.

****

A baby rabbit was orphaned. Fortunately though, a family of squirrels took it in and raised it as if it were one of their own. This adoption led to some peculiar behaviours on the part of the rabbit, including a tendency for it to eschew jumping but rather to embrace running around like its step-siblings. As the rabbit passed through puberty, however, it soon faced an identity crisis. It went to its foster-parents to discuss the problem. It explained how it felt different from its brothers and sisters, was unsure of its place in the universe, and was generally forlorn. The father squirrel just sat back and cracked another nut saying: "Don't scurry, be hoppy."

****

What's grey and puts out forest fires? Smoky the Elephant.

****

Why do ducks have flat feet? To stamp out forest fires.

****

Private Atkins joins the French Foreign Legion and is stationed at a remote outpost in the North African desert. After several weeks in barracks he feels a moist yearning for female companionship. He approaches the evil-looking, scar-faced sergeant, and asks him what the men do for sexual relief around here. "Zere eez only ze camel, oui?" the sergeant tells him with a leer. "I'm not desperate enough to brave that!" replies Atkins, and takes a brisk walk and another cold bath. A week later he's more desperate and asks the sergeant again. "Ze camel, I told you. Use ze camel!" comes the reply. Atkins actually has a look at the camel this time. It's like a flea-ridden carpet full of coat-hangers with camel shit matted in the hair round its rump. Atkins doesn't fancy it. Much. A week later, delirious with unvented lust he goes to the sergeant again, only to be told: "Merde! Ze camel I tell you, ze camel!" That night Atkins creeps out to the camel. "At least its got a pulse," he tells himself as he climbs onto a hay-rack and proceeds to roger the camel to his satisfaction. As he dismounts he sees the sergeant staring open-mouthed in horror and admiration. "How inventive and practical you Engleesh are. Ze other men, zey usually ride ze camel to ze brothel in town!"

****

Some veterinarians are prescribing Prozac for dogs. Animal rights activists are thrilled. Things have finally come full circle. Finally, a drug for animals that has been tested on humans first.

****

How does the male elephant find the female elephant when she's lying down in tall grass? Very attractive.

****

Why do elephants have four feet? Because lady elephants have big vaginas.

****

An old woman saved a fairy's life. To repay this, the fairy promised to grant the old woman three wishes. For the first wish, the old lady asked to become young and beautiful. Poof! She became young and beautiful. For the second wish, the old lady asked to be richest woman in the world. "Poof! She was the richest woman in the world. For the last wish, she pointed at the cat she had kept for years. She asked that he be turned into the most handsome man on earth. After all, he had been her best friend for so many years. Poof! The fairy turned the cat into the most handsome man on earth. The old lady and the fairy said their goodbyes. After the fairy left, the handsome man strolled over to her and asked: "Now aren't you sorry you had me neutered?"

****

Why is Turtle Wax so expensive? Because their ears are so small!

****

What is that stuff between elephants toes? Careless elephant drivers.

****

Why do elephants have Big Ears? Because Noddy won't pay the ransom.

****

A polar bear was out driving one day when he suddenly started having engine trouble. He pulled into the next service station and asked the walrus there to take a look at it. The walrus drove the car into the workshop and put it up on the hoist. After looking at it for a bit he returned and said to the polar bear, "You've blown a seal," to which the bear replied, "No, honestly! That's just mayonnaise from lunch."

****

A talent scout is walking down the street and comes across a man and his dog. The little dog is singing. He has a lovely voice and the talent scout says, "Come to my office. I want to sign you and this marvellous dog to a contract. This dog can make us both rich." The man brings his little dog to the talent scout's office. The little dog is just about to finish singing "La Donna E' Mobile", when a large dog runs into the room and grabs him by the scruff of the neck. She (it's a bitch) runs away with him in her mouth. The talent scout yells, "Stop her. She's taking away our fortune!" The man replies, sadly, "It's no use. That's his mother. She doesn't want him to be on stage. She wants him to be a doctor."

A man goes to a dog-breeder to buy a guard dog only to be presented with a scruffy terrier mongrel. "What use is that?" he asks. "Ah, but he's a trained killer, this one," promises the breeder. "Watch: Guard Dog? That chair!" In a blur of little snappy teeth and yapping the chair is reduced to splinters. "Amazing!" says the man. "Can I have a go? Guard Dog? That box!" In seconds the box is shredded to mere fluff. Delighted, he buys the mutt and rushes home to show his lady wife. "Look at our new guard dog," he says. "He's a trained killer!" "What that thing?" she replies. "Guard dog, my arse!"

****

Wife: "We've got such a clever dog. He brings in the daily newspapers every morning." Husband: "Well, lots of dogs can do that." " Wife: "But we've never subscribed to any papers."

****

How do you make a dog go meow? Freeze it in liquid nitrogen, then take a chainsaw to it.

****

A man went to a doctor to have his penis enlarged. Well, this particular procedure involved grafting a baby elephant's trunk onto the man's penis. Overjoyed, the man went out with his best girl to a very fancy restaurant. After cocktails, the man's penis crept out of his pants, felt around the table, grabbed a bread roll and quickly disappeared under the tablecloth. The girl was startled and exclaimed: "What was that?" Suddenly, the penis came back, took another bread roll and just as quickly disappeared. The girl was silent for a moment, then finally said: "I don't believe I saw what I think I just saw...can you do that again?" With a strained smile the man replied: "Darling, I'd like to, but I don't think my arse can take another bread roll!"

****

How do you make a dead elephant float? Well, you take ten dead elephants, ten tons of chocolate ice-cream, five tons of bananas...

****

"No!" said the lady millipede, crossing her legs, "no, a thousand times no!"

****

There was a herd of cattle all standing on a hill when an earthquake struck. All of the cows fell down, but the bull remained standing. The farmer noticing this went out and asked the bull, "Why didn't you fall down like the rest of the herd. The bull replied: "We bulls wobble, but we don't fall over."

Why did the Iraqi chicken cross the road? To take over the other side.

****

Why did the chicken cross the road again? Because it was a double-crosser.

****

Why do pygmies wear giant condoms on their heads? Because if an elephant steps on them, they're fucked!

****

A farmer with lots of chickens posted the following sign: "Free Chickens. Our Coop Runneth Over."

****

Men and women have been calling to fish, pleading with them, and swearing at them without response since the beginning of time. Scientists have set out to translate fish language. They are not far along yet, but have made some headway. Various clicks and whistles have been recorded that indicate that one fish has a way to communicate what is on his mind to another fish. If the research continues as planned, it should be only a matter of time until man will be able to reproduce fish noises and communicate what is on his mind to bass, perch, and catfish. All right-minded fishermen agree that fish-talk research projects should be cancelled and the scientists on them forced to seek other employment. The reasoning behind this point of view is simple and sound. If the research continues to its logical conclusion, fishing will cease to be the pleasant and relaxing sport that it now is. Fishing will become a business of bellowing speeches in fish language designed to convince fish that they would be better off on the bank or in the boat than they are in the water. In such circumstances, any fool knows who the men who'll catch all the fish will be... They'll be politicians.

****

"What is it, Lassie? A boy fell down a mine shaft and broke his ankle and is diabetic and needs insulin? Is THAT what you're trying to tell me?"

****

A Norwich University professor has been studying cow flatulence for 20 years, and has determined that the average cow emits 200 to 400 litres of methane gas PER DAY, resulting in a total annual world cow methane output of 50 million metric TONS! This is why you should never allow a cow inside your sleeping bag!!

Why couldn't the pony talk? Because he was a little hoarse.

****

A man went to visit a friend and was amazed to find him playing chess with his dog. "I can hardly believe my eyes!" he exclaimed. "That's the smartest dog I've ever seen." "Oh, he's not so clever," the friend replied, "I've beaten him three games out of five."

****

Once upon a time, there was a non-conforming sparrow who decided not to fly south for the winter. However, soon after the weather turned cold, the sparrow changed his mind and reluctantly started to fly south. After a short time, ice began to form his on his wings and he fell to earth in a barnyard almost frozen. A cow passed by and crapped on this little bird and the sparrow thought it was the end, but the manure warmed him and defrosted his wings. Warm and happy the little sparrow began to sing. Just then, a large Tom cat came by and hearing the chirping investigated the sounds. As Old Tom cleared away the manure, he found the chirping bird and promptly ate him. There are three morals to this story: 1) Everyone who shits on you is not necessarily your enemy. 2) Everyone who gets you out of shit is not necessarily your friend. 3) If you are warm and happy in a pile of shit, keep your silly beak shut.

The After-Work Crowd

2

Jokes about Jobs, Bosses and Lawyers

Mr Matthews sat in his attorney's office. "Do you want the bad news first or the terrible news?" the lawyer said. "Give me the bad news first." "Your wife found a picture worth a half-million dollars." "That's the bad news?" asked Matthews incredulously. "I can't wait to hear the terrible news." "The terrible news is that it's of you and your secretary."

****

Work hard and save your money and when you are old you will be able to buy the things only the young can enjoy.

****

When Willie retired from the railway after 50 years' service, the company presented him with an old coach to keep in his garden as a memento. One wet day, his friends found him sitting on the step of the coach, smoking his pipe with an old sack over his shoulders to keep out the rain. "Hullo, Willie," said his pals, "why are ye no' inside on a day like this?" "Can ye no' see," replied Willie, with a nod toward the coach. "They sent me a non-smoker."

****

How can you tell if your barrister is worthless? Ask him if he's a member of the bar.

I worry all the time: I worry about worrying too much. I worry when I'm not worried that there's something I should be worried about. I worry when I'm worried whether I should worry about what I am currently worried about or whether I should worry about something else that worries me, even if I'm not worried about it, but should be worried about it or at least worry about the fact that I'm worrying about not possibly having to worry at all, about worrying.

****

A lawyer was trying to console a weeping widow. Her husband had passed away without a will. "Did the deceased have any last words?" asked the lawyer. "You mean right before he died?" sobbed the widow. "Yes," replied the lawyer, "they might be helpful if it's not too painful for you to recall." "Well," she began, "he said 'Don't try to scare me. You couldn't hit the broad side of a barn with that gun.'"

****

If you see a lawyer on a bicycle, why don't you swerve to hit him? It might be your bicycle.

****

A president of a democracy is a man who is always ready, willing, and able to lay down your life for his country.

A nun is undressing for a bath and while she's standing naked, there's a knock at the door. The nun calls, "who is it?" A voice answers, "Aablind salesman." The nun decides to get a thrill by having the blind man in the room while she's naked, so she lets him in. The man walks in, looks straight at the nun and says: "Uhhhh, well hello there, where would you be wanting the blinds fitted...?"

****

If you perceive that there are four possible ways in which a procedure can go wrong and circumvent these, then a fifth way, unprepared for, will promptly develop.

****

The merchandizing manager of a large food chain was on holiday. While driving through rural Norfolk he developed a headache and decided to stop in the next town and buy some aspirin. Stopping at a small grocery store, he went in and got his aspirin. While in the store, more out of habit than anything, he walked around to see how it was merchandized. To his amazement, only about two of the ten aisles in the store were devoted to the basic staples and the other eight aisles were filled with salt. He had never seen anything like this in his life and wondered what caused this huge demand for salt in a small rural town in Norfolk. Seeing the proprietor in the rear of the store he said, "My God, you sell a lot of salt." At which the owner said: "Who me?

Wurr, boy. I don't 'ardly sell any salt at all, but that fellow that sells me salt, does he know how to sell salt."

****

Why should lawyers wear lots of sunscreen when holidaying at a beach resort? Because they're used to doing all of their lying indoors.

****

He who beats his sword into a plowshare usually ends up plowing for those who kept their swords.

****

Diplomacy is the art of saying "nice doggy" until you find a large enough rock.

****

A very large department store chain in the UK is very low on sales. The head of personnel, Mr Jones, informs the head of each department store that they are to send all employees over the age of 60 out on early pension. The early pension plan is implemented. After three months, Mr Jones, in going over store reports, notices that the Croydon store has an employee over the age of 60. Mr Jones calls

Mr Smith at the Croydon branch to find out why Mr Green is still with the firm. Mr Smith explains to Mr Jones that Mr Green is the best salesman that the store has ever had. He brings hundreds of thousands of pounds into the shop a year – to let him go would be a real loss. The following week, Mr Jones goes to the shop and down to the sales floor to secretly watch Mr Green in action. Mr Green says to a customer: "You know, with that new fishing rod that you bought, you should really have some new fishing clothes." The customer is convinced and Mr Green outfits him in hundreds of pounds worth of new fishing clothes. Mr Green continues: "You know, you are going to look so spiffy in that new outfit with your new fishing rod that it would be a pity not to be seen. Instead of just standing on the banks of the river, you should be seen in a new fishing boat." The customer is convinced and Mr Green sells him a new fishing boat. Mr Green is so convincing that he also sells the customer a new boat trailer and a new car to go along with the new boat, new outfit, and new fishing rod. By the time the sale is rung up, Mr Green has sold thousands and thousands of pounds worth of merchandise. Mr Jones is absolutely astounded. He tells Mr Smith to give Mr Green a raise. He says to Mr Smith, "I have never seen such an outstanding selling job in my life. It is unbelievable that the customer came in for a simple fishing rod and Mr Green sold him thousands of pounds worth of merchandize." Mr Smith says: "That's not even the beautiful part. That customer didn't even come in for a fishing rod. He came in to buy his wife a box of tampons. Mr Green convinced him that since his weekend was already shot, he may as well go fishing..."

The scene is a dark jungle in Africa. Two tigers are stalking through the brush when the one to the rear reaches out with his tongue and licks the arse of the tiger in front. The startled tiger turns around and says: "Hey, leave it out, alright?" The rear tiger says, "sorry", and they continue. After about another five minutes, the rear tiger again reaches out with his tongue and licks the arse of the tiger in front. The front tiger turns around and cuffs the rear tiger and says: "I said stop it!" The rear tiger says, "sorry", and they continue. After about another five minutes, the rear tiger once more licks the arse of the tiger in front. The front tiger turns around and asks the rear tiger: "What is it with you, anyway?" The rear tiger replies: "Well, I just ate a lawyer and I'm trying to get the taste out of my mouth."

****

We need either less corruption or more chance to participate in it.

****

Between the pigeons and the politicians, it's hard to keep the courthouse clean.

****

A travelling salesman stops at a petrol station to take a crap. The toilet has two stalls and there's a man already there using one of them. The two men acknowledge each other and go about their business. The salesman finishes first and, as he pulls his trousers up, some coins drop into the toilet bowl. He looks at it, thinks for a moment and throws £20 note into the bowl. The other man, astonished, asks: "Why the hell did you do that?" The salesman says: "You don't expect me to put my hand in there for 35 pence do you?."

****

A conclusion is the place where you got tired of thinking.

****

By the time you can make ends meet, they've moved the ends.

****

Lawyers are the only profession where the more there are, the more are needed.

****

A man goes to an office and sees a crying secretary. "Excuse me, but what is the matter with you?" "My boss told me that I am not pretty enough to make so many typing errors..."

Where can you find a good lawyer? In the cemetery.

****

A man walks into a department store, finds the manager and says, "I really need a job, how about giving me a chance?" Manager says, "Certainly, but you have to sell these 500 toothbrushes in a week to get the job." Our hero takes the toothbrushes and leaves. Next week, he comes back with the toothbrushes and finds the manager. "I didn't get any of these sold, but please, please, give me another chance." Manager says, "Ok, but you have to take another 500 toothbrushes." Our man takes the toothbrushes and tries his luck again. Again our man comes back with the 1000 toothbrushes, talks to the manager, gets another 500 toothbrushes and tries his luck... So he comes back in a week, not with 1500 toothbrushes but with a bag of money. The manager gives him the job and wants to know his trick. Our hero says: "Well, the idea came to me a couple of days ago. I set up a table on a busy street corner with a bowl of chips, a bowl of shit, and a sign saying 'Free Chip and Dip'. Someone would come along, dip the chip, and say, 'Yuck! That tastes like shit.' and, of course, I would reply, 'Yeah. So, want to buy a toothbrush?'"

****

The easiest way to find something lost around the office is to buy a replacement.

There were two grocers, Smith and Jones, in the same street. Smith had a sign in his window, "Avocados, 20 pence a pound". A woman goes in and asks for some. "Sorry love", said Smith, I haven't got any in just now. Come back on Wednesday." So she goes on up the street to Jones' shop. His avocados are £2.50 a pound, but at least he has them in stock. "That's a bit steep isn't it? Smith's are only 20 pence a pound." "Yeah," says Jones, "so are mine when I'm out of stock."

****

I broke a mirror in my house. I'm supposed to get seven years of bad luck, but my lawyer thinks he can get me five.

****

The unemployment rate is so bad in Birmingham that when a post office posted a notice reading "WANTED for Armed Robbery", 25 people responded.

****

Did you hear about the new sushi bar that caters exclusively to lawyers? It's called Sosumi.

****

When the Lord made man, all the parts of the body argued over who would be boss. The brain explained that since he controlled all the parts of the body, he should be boss. The legs argued that since they took the man wherever he wanted to go, they should be boss. The stomach suggested that since he digests all the food, he should be boss. The eyes said that without them man would be helpless, so they should be boss. And so it went on. The hands, heart, ears, and lungs each demanded that they be made boss. Then the arsehole applied for the job, but the other parts just laughed, so the arsehole became mad and closed up. After a few days, the brain went foggy, the legs got wobbly, the stomach got ill, and the eyes got crossed and unable to see. They all conceded and made the arsehole boss. This proves that you don't have to be a brain to be a boss, just an arsehole

****

A fool and his money are soon elected.

****

When a lawyer tells his clients he has a sliding fee schedule what he means is that after he bills you it's financially hard to get back on your feet.

****

An airliner was having engine trouble and the pilot instructed the cabin crew to have the passengers take their seats and prepare for an emergency landing. A few minutes later, the pilot asked the flight attendants if everyone was buckled in and ready. "All set back here, Captain," came the reply, "except one lawyer who is still passing out business cards."

****

There was the cartoon showing two people fighting over a cow. One was pulling the cow by the tail; the other was pulling on the horns. Underneath was a lawyer milking the cow.

****

A doctor, an engineer, and a lawyer go out hunting in the woods one day. Each of them brings along his hunting dog, and they spend most of the morning arguing about which of the dogs is the smartest. Early in the afternoon, they discover a clearing in the forest. In the middle of the clearing is a large pile of animal bones. Seeing the bones, the doctor turns to the others and says: "I'm going to prove to you two that my dog is the smartest. Watch this." He then calls his dog over and says: "Bones. See the bones? Go get 'em." The dog rushes over to the pile, rummages around for a bit, and then proceeds to build a replica of the human skeleton, perfect down to the last detail. The doctor grins smugly; after all, his dog has just built a human skeleton from animal bones. The engineer, however, is totally unimpressed. "That's nothing," he says. "Watch this." He calls his dog over, and points out the pile. "Bones. Get the bones." The dog rushes over, tears down the skeleton, and in its place builds a perfect replica of the Eiffel Tower. It even has a little French flag waving at the top. The doctor is forced to agree that the engineer's dog is, in fact, smarter than his own. The lawyer, however, is still not impressed. "My dog is smarter," he says. "Watch." He then calls his dog over, points to the pile, and says simply "Bones." The dog rushes over to the pile, tears down the tower, eats half the bones, buries the other half, screws the other two dogs, and takes the rest of the afternoon off.

****

Between grand theft and a legal fee, there only stands a law degree.

****

What is brown and black and looks good on a lawyer? A Doberman.

****

A couple of months in the lab can often save a couple of hours in the library.

****

As productivity has not increased since the implementation of the seven-day working week, the stoppage of all company health and retirement plans, the 20 per cent pay cut, the ten-year pay freeze, the installation of video cameras in company restrooms, the hiring of the corporate truant officers to check up on all employees calling in sick, and the random drug and dirty underwear screenings, management has decided that the beatings and mandatory self-flagellations will continue until morale improves.

****

What do you call an honest lawyer? Hypothetical.

****

Creativity is great, but plagiarism is faster.

****

Artificial intelligence usually beats real stupidity.

****

Never volunteer for anything.

Have you heard about the lawyers' word processor? No matter what font or typesize you select, everything come out in fine print.

****

Experience is what causes a person to make new mistakes instead of old ones.

****

A car company is planning to build a new model made from all its previous engineering errors. The new model will be called Total Recall.

****

A fellow had just been hired as the new managing director of a large high tech corporation. The managing director who was stepping down, met with him privately and presented him with three numbered envelopes. "Open these if you run up against a problem you don't think you can solve," he said. Well, things went along pretty smoothly, but six months later, sales took a downturn and the new MD was really catching a lot of heat. About at his wits's end, he remembered the envelopes. He went to his drawer and took out the first envelope. The message read, "Blame your predecessor." The new MD called a press conference and tactfully laid the blame at the feet of the previous MD. Satisfied with his comments, the press – and The City responded positively, sales began to pick up and the problem was soon behind him. About a year later, the company was again experiencing a slight dip in sales, combined with serious product problems. Having learned from his previous experience, the MD quickly opened the second envelope. The message read, "Reorganize." This he did, and the company quickly rebounded. After several consecutive profitable quarters, the company once again fell on difficult times. The MD went to his office, closed the door and opened the third envelope. The message said: "Prepare three envelopes."

****

What did the harassed lawyer say? Get off my case.

****

The boss returned from lunch in a good mood and called the whole staff in to listen to a couple of jokes he had picked up. Everybody but one girl laughed uproariously. "What's the matter?" grumbled the boss. "Haven't you got a sense of humour?" "I don't have to laugh," she said, "I'm leaving on Friday."

****

When angry, count to ten before you speak. If VERY angry, count to 100, and then go and shout at someone junior.

****

What do you call a lawyer with an IQ of 50? Your Honour.

****

Secretary: "I would like to inform you that I have found a new position." Boss: "Fine, what are we waiting for, let's try it."

****

In front of you stand four men: Adolf Hitler, Idi Amin, Saddam Hussein and a lawyer. You are holding a gun which contains only three bullets. Who do you shoot? Use all three bullets on the lawyer. Its the only way to be sure.

****

"You are a cheat," shouted the attorney to his opponent. "And you're a liar," bellowed the opposition. Banging his gavel sharply, his Honour interrupted: "All right, now that both barristers have been identified, let's get on with this case."

A door-to-door vacuum cleaner salesman manages to bullshit his way into a woman's home in outback Australia. "This machine is the best ever," he claims, while pouring a bag of dirt over the lounge floor. The woman says she's really worried it may not all come off, so the salesman says: "If this machine doesn't remove all the dust completely, I'll lick it off myself." "Do you want ketchup. We're not connected to the electricity yet."

****

A businessman was having a tough time lugging his lumpy, oversized suitcase on to the plane. Helped by a stewardess, he finally managed to stuff it in the overhead locker. "Do you always carry such heavy luggage?" she sighed. "No more," the man replied. "Next time, I'm riding in the bag, and my partner can buy the ticket."

****

Take heart, the only person who always got his work done by Friday was Robinson Crusoe.

****

A circuit-judge in a small-town court was hearing a drunk-driving case and the defendant, who had both a record and a reputation for driving under the influence, demanded a jury trial. It was nearly 4pm.

And getting a jury would take time, so the judge called a recess and went out in the hall looking to empanel anyone available for jury duty. He found a dozen lawyers in the main lobby and told them that they were a jury. The lawyers thought this would be a novel experience and so followed the judge back to the courtroom. The trial was over in about ten minutes and it was very clear that the defendant was guilty. The jury went into the jury room, the judge started getting ready to go home, and everyone waited. After nearly three hours, the judge was totally out of patience and sent the usher into the jury room to see what was holding up the verdict. When the usher returned, the judge said: "Well have they got a verdict yet?" The usher shook his head and said: "Verdict? No M'lud, they're still doing nominating speeches for the foreman's position."

****

A speaker was getting tired of being interrupted. He grabbed the microphone and said loudly, "We seem to have a great many fools here tonight. Would it be advisable to hear one at a time?" Someone in the back of the room said, "Yes. Get on with the speech."

****

Diplomacy is the art of letting someone else have your way.

****

It has been reported in a magazine that a certain cosmetics company has more than 36,000 sales representatives in the Amazonia region of Brazil, with sales growing at 50 per cent a year. The company representatives in Amazonia sell the complete range of products, from lipstick, moisturizer, and mascara to men's bikini briefs, and accept for payment almost any barterable items, such as fish.

****

A man on trial at the Old Bailey had previously pleaded "not guilty". However, once the jury, eight women and four men, had been seated and the trial was under way, the defendant switched his plea. "Why the change?" asked the judge. "Were you persuaded to plead 'guilty'?" "No Sir," the man replied, "when I pleaded 'not guilty', I didn't know women would be on the jury. I can't fool one woman, so I know I can't fool eight of them."

****

What do you get when you cross the Godfather with a lawyer? An offer you can't understand.

****

A lawyer named Strange was shopping for a gravestone. After he had made his selection, the stonemason asked him what inscription he would like on it. "Here lies an honest man and a lawyer," responded the lawyer. "Sorry, but I can't do that," replied the stonecutter. "In this country, it's against the law to bury two people in the same grave. However, I could put 'here lies an honest lawyer'" "But that won't let people know who it is" protested the lawyer. "Certainly will," retorted the stonecutter. "People will read it and exclaim, 'That's strange.'"

****

How do you know when your divorce is getting ugly? When your lawyer doesn't seem like the bloodsucking leech anymore.

****

Why did the lawyer cross the road? To get to the car accident on the other side.

****

A lawyer died and appeared before the pearly gates. When he arrived, a chorus of angels began to sing in his honour and St Peter himself came out to shake his hand. "Mr Morris," said St Peter, "it is a great honour to have you here at last. You are the first being to break Methuselah's record for longevity. You have lived 1028 years." "What are you talking about?" said Morris. "I'm 56." "56? But aren't you John Morris?" "Yes." "A lawyer?" "Yes." "From Knightsbridge?"

"Yes." "Let me check the records," said St Peter. He slapped his hand against his forehead. "Now I see the mistake, we added up your billing hours."

****

A new employee was habitually late. Finally, the foreman called him in. "Don't you know what time we go to work here?" he shouted. "No, sir," was the reply, "I haven't been able to work it out yet, because the rest of you are always already here."

****

Sam Cohen, father of three and faithful husband for over 40 years, unexpectedly drops dead one day. His lawyer informs his widow that Stu Schwartz, Sam's best friend since childhood, is to be executor of the will. The day comes to divide Sam's earthly possessions – over a million pounds' worth. In front of Sam's family, Stu reads the will: "Stu, if you're reading this, then I must be dead. You were such a good friend for so long, how can I ignore you in this will? On the other hand, there are my beloved Sophie and my children to be looked after. Stu, I know you can make sure my family is taken care of properly. So Stu, give what you want to her and take the rest for yourself." Stu then looks at the survivors and tells them that, in accordance with Sam's instructions, he will give fifty thousand pounds to Sam's widow. The rest he is retaining for himself. The family is beside itself. "This is impossible. Forty years of marriage and then this? It can't be." So the family sues. Their day in court arrives, and after testimony from both sides, the judge gives his verdict: "To Stuart Schwartz, I award fifty thousand pounds of the contested money. The remainder shall go to Sophie Cohen, widow of the deceased." Needless to say, the family is elated, but Stu is dumbfound. "Your Honour, how can you do this? The will made Sam's wishes quite clear: 'Give what you want to her and take the rest for yourself.' I wanted the lion's share. What gives?" The judge answered back, "Mr Schwartz, Sam Cohen knew you his whole life. He wanted to give you something in gratitude. He also wanted to see his family taken care of. So he drew up his will accordingly. But you misread his instructions. You see, Sam knew just what kind of a person you are, so with his family's interest in mind, he didn't say, 'give what you want to her and keep the rest for yourself.' No. What Sam said was, 'Give what YOU want to HER; and keep the rest for yourself'."

****

This executive was interviewing a nervous young women for a position in his company. He wanted to find out something about her personality so he asked, "If you could have a conversation with someone, living or dead, who would it be?" The girl quickly responded, "the living one."

I'll share with you my own secret method for moving up the corporate ladder. It's called the Hind-lick Manoeuvre.

****

In order to get a loan, you must first prove you don't need it.

****

When I first started working, I used to dream of the day when I might be earning the salary I'm starving on now.

****

Lawyers are people who can write a ten-thousand-word document and call it a brief.

****

At the funeral of a lady was her doctor, a friend and her lawyer. Each had promised her that at her funeral they would toss £1000 into her grave. The doctor and friend each tossed in their £1000 cash, after which the lawyer removed the cash and placed a cheque for £3000.

****

The president of a large corporation opened his directors meeting by announcing: "All those who are opposed to the plan I am about to propose will reply by saying, 'I resign.'"

****

Prosecutor: "Did you kill the victim?" Defendant: "No, I did not." Prosecutor: "Do you know what the penalties are for perjury?" Defendant: "Yes, I do. And they're a hell of a lot better than the penalty for murder."

****

A man was walking down the street one day and he saw a "Salesman Wanted" sign in a window. He went in the store and the owner asked, "Can I help you?" "I'I'IIII w'w'waannnttt j'j'jjoooobbbb," said the man. "I don't know if this job would suit you because of your speaking problem," said the owner. "I'I'III h'h'avvee a'a'a wif'f'fe annd si' si' six k'k'ids a'a'ndd I'I n'neeeed th'th'e j'joobb," said the man. "Okay, here are three Bibles. Go out and sell them," said the owner. So the man went out and came back an hour later. "H'here'sss your mm'money," said the man. The owner was impressed, so he gave the man a dozen more Bibles and sent him out. The man came back in two hours and said, "H'here'sss your mm'money." The owner said, "This is fantastic. You sold more Bibles in three hours than anyone has sold in a week. Tell me, what do you say to the people when they come to the door?" "W'welll," said the man, "III r'r'ing the d'd'oor b'b'ell a'a'nd s's'say 'M'M'aaddammm, d'd'o y'y'ou w'w'ant t'to b'buy t'this B'Bible o'o'rrr d'd'o y'you w'w'w'ant m'me t't'o read it to you?'"

****

Why do lawyers carry their certification on their dashboard? So they can park in the handicapped parking; it's proof of a moral disability.

****

A man walked into a bar with his crocodile and asked the bartender: "Do you serve lawyers here?" "Certainly," replied the bartender. "Good," said the man. "Give me a beer, and I'll have a lawyer for my croc."

****

The son of a Spanish lawyer graduated from college and was considering the future. He went to his father, who had a very large office, and asked if he might be given a desk in the corner where he could observe his father's activities. He could be introduced to his father's clients as a clerk. That way, he could decide on whether or not to become a lawyer. His father thought this a splendid idea and this arrangement was set up immediately. On his son's first day at work, the first client in the morning was a rough-hewn man with calloused hands, in workman's attire, who began the conversation by saying: "Mr Lawyer, I work for some people named Gonzales who have a ranch on the east side of town. For many years, I have tended their crops and animals, including some cows. I have raised the cows, tended them, fed them, and it has always been my understanding and belief that I was the owner of the cows. Mr Gonzales died and his son has inherited the farm, and he believes that since the cows were raised on his ranch and fed on his hay, the cows are his. In short, we have a dispute as to the ownership of the cows." The lawyer said: "I have heard enough. I will take your case. DON'T WORRY ABOUT THE COWS." After the tenant farmer left, the next client came in, a young, well-dressed man, clearly a member of the landed class. "My name is Gonzales. I own a farm on the east side of the town," he said. "For many years, a tenant farmer has worked for my family tending the crops and animals, including some cows. The cows have been raised on my land and fed on my hay, and I believe that they belong to me, but the tenant farmer believes that since he raised them and cared for them, they are his. In short, we have a dispute over ownership of the cows." The lawyer said, "I have heard enough. I will take your case. DON'T WORRY ABOUT THE COWS." After the client left, the son came over to his father with a look of concern. "My father, I know nothing of the law, but it seems to me that we have a serious problem regarding these cows." "DON'T WORRY ABOUT THE COWS." said the lawyer. "The cows will be ours."

A little old lady walked into the head branch of a respected bank holding a large paper bag in her hand. She told the young man at the window that she wished to take the £3 million she had in the bag and open an account with the bank. As it was such a large sum she asked to meet the manager of the bank first. The teller seemed to think that was a reasonable request and after opening the paper bag and seeing the bundles of £50 notes, which amounted to around £3 million, he telephoned the manager's secretary to arrange this. The lady was escorted upstairs and ushered into the manager's office. Introductions were made and the lady stated that she would like to get to know the people she did business with on a more personal level. The bank manager then asked her where she came into such a large amount of money. "Was it an inheritance?" he asked. "No," she answered. "Was it from playing the stock market?" "No," she replied. He was quiet for a minute, trying to think of where this little old lady could possibly come into £3 million. "I bet on things," she stated. "You bet?" repeated the bank manager, "as in horses?" "No," she replied, "I bet people." Seeing his confusion, she explained that she just bet different things with people. All of a sudden she said, "I'll bet you £25,000 that by ten o'clock tomorrow morning, your balls will be square." The bank manager figured she must be off her rocker and decided to take her up on the bet. He didn't see how he could lose. For the rest of the day, the bank manager was very careful. He decided to stay home that evening and take no chances; there was £25,000 at stake. When he got up in the morning and took his shower, he checked to make sure everything was okay. There was no difference; he looked the same as he always had. He went to work and waited for the little old lady to come in at ten o'clock, humming as he went. He knew this would be a good day; how often do you get handed £25,000 for doing nothing? At ten o'clock sharp, the little old lady was shown into his office. With her was a younger man. When he inquired as to the man's purpose for being there, she informed him that he was her lawyer and she always took him along when there was this much money involved. "Well?" she asked, "what about our bet?" "I don't know how to tell you this," he replied, "but I am the same as I've always been only £25,000 richer." The lady seemed to accept this, but requested that she be able to see for herself. The bank manager thought this was reasonable and dropped his trousers. She instructed him to bend over and then grabbed a hold of him. Sure enough, everything was fine. The bank manager then looked up and saw her lawyer standing across the room banging his head against the wall. "What's wrong with him?" he inquired. "Oh him," she replied," I bet him £100,000 that by ten o'clock this morning that I'd have the bank manager by the bollocks."

****

If a lawyer and a tax inspector were both drowning, and you could only save one of them, would you go to lunch or read the paper?

****

Once overheard at the office water cooler: "The boss said that I would get a raise when I earned it. He's crazy if he thinks I'm gonna wait that long."

****

A man, who barely made it through the Black Monday stock-market crash, called his stockbrokers the next day and asked, "May I speak to Mr Spencer please?" The operator replied, "I'm sorry. Mr Spencer is deceased. Can anyone else help you?" The man said "no" and hung up. Ten minutes later, he called again and asked for Mr Spencer, his broker. The operator said, "You just called a few minutes ago, didn't you? Mr Spencer has died. I'm not making this up." The man again hung up. Fifteen minutes later he called a third time and asked for Mr Spencer. The operator was irked by this time. "I've told you twice already, Mr Spencer is dead. He is not here. Why do you keep asking for him when I say he's dead?" The man replied: "I just like hearing it."

****

You Know It Is Going To Be A Bad Day At Work When... The gypsy fortune-teller offers to refund your money.

****

What is the ideal weight of a lawyer? About three pounds, including the urn.

****

Experts are people who know a great deal about very little and who go along learning more and more about less and less until they know practically everything about nothing. Lawyers, on the other hand, are people who know very little about many things and keep learning less and less about more and more until they know practically nothing about everything. Judges are people who start out knowing everything about everything but end up knowing nothing about anything because of their constant association with experts and lawyers.

****

It seems that a devout, good couple was about to get married, but a tragic car accident ended their lives. When they got to heaven, they asked St Peter if he could arrange for them to be married, saying that it was what they had hoped for in life, and they still desired wedded union. He thought about it and agreed, but said they would have to wait. It was almost one hundred years later when St Peter sent for them. They were married in a simple ceremony. So things went on, for thirty years or so, but they determined, in this time, that eternity was best not spent together. They went back to St Peter, and said, "We thought we would be happy forever, but now we believe that we have irreconcilable differences. Is there any way we can get divorced?" "Are you kidding?" said St Peter. "It took me a hundred years to get a priest up here to marry you. I'll never get a lawyer."

****

Why didn't the mime artist feel so bad about his career? At least he wasn't a lawyer.

****

All work and no play will make you a manager.

****

How do you get a lawyer out of a tree? Cut the rope.

****

How many lawyers does it take to stop a moving bus? Never enough.

****

What is the difference between a lawyer and a skunk? Nobody wants to hit a skunk.

In a terrible accident at a railroad crossing, a train smashed into a car and pushed it nearly 400 yards down the track. Though no one was killed, the driver took the train company to court. At the trial, the engineer insisted that he had given the driver ample warning by waving his lantern back and forth for nearly a minute. He even stood and convincingly demonstrated how he'd done it. The court believed his story and the suit was dismissed. "Congratulations," the lawyer said to the engineer when it was over, "you did superbly under cross-examination." "Thanks," he said, "but he sure had me worried." "How's that?" the lawyer asked. "I was afraid he was going to ask if the lantern was lit."

****

Q: How many lawyers does it take to change a light bulb? A: Such number as may be deemed necessary to perform the stated task in a timely and efficient manner within the strictures of the following agreement: Whereas the party of the first part, also known as "Lawyer", and the party of the second part, also known as "Light Bulb", do hereby and forthwith agree to a transaction wherein the party of the second part (Light Bulb) shall be removed from the current position as a result of failure to perform previously agreed upon duties, ie: the lighting, elucidation, and otherwise illumination of the area ranging from the front (north) door, through the entryway, terminating at an area just inside the primary living area, demarcated by the beginning of the carpet, any spillover illumination being at the option of the party of the second part (Light Bulb) and not required by the aforementioned agreement between the parties. The aforementioned removal transaction shall include, but not be limited to, the following steps: 1) The party of the first part (Lawyer) shall, with or without elevation at his option, by means of a chair, stepstool, ladder or any other means of elevation, grasp the party of the second part (Light Bulb) and rotate the party of the second part (Light Bulb) in a counter-clockwise direction, this point being non-negotiable. 2) Upon reaching a point where the party of the second part (Light Bulb) becomes separated from the party of the third part (Receptacle), the party of the first part (Lawyer) shall have the option of disposing of the party of the second part (Light Bulb) in a manner consistent with all applicable European, local and Government statutes. 3) Once separation and disposal have been achieved, the party of the first part (Lawyer) shall have the option of beginning installation of the party of the fourth part (New Light Bulb). This installation shall occur in a manner consistent with the reverse of the procedures described in step one of this self-same document, being careful to note that the rotation should occur in a clockwise direction, this point also being non-negotiable. Note: The above described steps may be performed, at the option of the party of the first part (Lawyer), by any or all persons authorized by him, the objective being to produce the most possible revenue for the party of the fifth part, also known as "Partnership". Charge: £2185.

****

A man went into the Town Hall of a small town, obviously desperate. He asked the man at the counter, "Is there a criminal lawyer in town?" The man replied: "Yes, but we can't prove it yet."

****

What do you call a person who assists a criminal in breaking the law before the criminal gets arrested? An accomplice. What do you call a person who assists a criminal in breaking the law after the criminal gets arrested? A lawyer.

****

How do you kill four thousand lawyers? You build a new Titanic and declare it cannot sink.

****

What is the difference between a lawyer and a herd of buffalo? The lawyer charges more.

****

If only one price can be obtained for a quotation, the price will be unreasonable.

Doctor's Orders

3

Jokes about Doctors and their kind

Two country doctors out in the Yorkshire Dales were discussing the population explosion in the world. One physician said: "Why, at t'current rate o' population growth, there'll soon be no'but standing room on t'whole planet." After a thoughtful pause, the other doctor replied, "Aye, but that'll slow t'buggers down a bit."

****

Patient: "Well, doctor, what does the X-ray of my head show?"
Doctor: "Absolutely nothing."

****

A guy goes to the doctor with a mysterious pain and tells the doctor, "Doc, Doc, my penis has been burning lately." And the doctor says reassuringly, "Don't worry son, that just means someone is talking about it."

****

A woman goes to a doctor with a problem. She's sitting on the chair next to the doctor, and she's very hesitant about describing her problem. Eventually, the doctor manages to discover that she thinks she may be sexually perverted. "What sort of perversion are you talking about?" asks the doctor. "Well," says the woman, "I like to be... Ohh... Ah... Ummm... I'm sorry doctor, but I'm too ashamed to talk about it." "Come, come, my dear. I'm a doctor you know; I've been trained to understand these problems. So what's the matter...?" So the woman again tries to explain, but gets so embarrassed that she just turns bright red and looks as though she might faint. Then the doctor has a bright idea. "Look," he says, "I'm a bit of a pervert myself. So if you show me what your perversion is, I'll show you what mine is. Okay? Is it a deal?" The woman considers the offer and after a short while agrees that it's a fair request. So after a slight pause, she says: "Well my perversion is... My perversion... Oh... I like to be kissed on the bottom." "Shit, is that ALL," says the doctor. "Look, go behind that screen, take all your clothes off, and I'll come round and show you what MY perversion is." So the woman does as she is told and undresses behind the screen. She gets down on all fours thinking to herself, "Hmmmm, perhaps he might kiss me on the bottom." Anyway, 15 minutes pass and nothing has happened. So the woman peers around the side of the screen to see the doctor sitting behind his desk, his feet up on the table, reading a newspaper and whistling to himself. "Hey!" shouts the woman, "I thought you said you were a pervert?" "Oh I am," says the doctor, "I've just crapped in your handbag."

****

Be a better psychiatrist and the world will beat a psychopath to your door.

What do you call a man who ignores doctors' advice? The Health Secretary.

****

A woman goes to her doctor who verifies that she is pregnant. This is her first pregnancy. The doctor asks her if she has any questions. She replies, "Well, I'm a little worried about the pain. How much will childbirth hurt?" The doctor answers, "Well, that varies from woman to woman and pregnancy to pregnancy and besides, it's difficult to describe pain." "I know, but can't you give me some idea?" she asks. "Grab your upper lip and pull it out a little..." "Like this?" "A little more..." "Like this?" "No. A little more..." "Like this?" "Yes. Does that hurt?" "A little bit." "Now stretch it over your head."

****

Did you hear about the doctor who had his licence taken away because he was having affairs with his patients? Yes, it's a shame because he was one of the top veterinarians in the country.

****

A young woman, two months pregnant, went to see her obstetrician. He was in a hurry to leave on an emergency call, so he asked her to quickly bare her stomach, then reached into his desk and took out a rubber stamp, which he pressed beside her navel. He then rushed off. At home, she and her husband tried to read the tiny words printed on her belly, but they were too small. They then found a magnifying glass and tried to read the words. The stamp read: "When your husband can read this without his glasses, it's time to get yourself to the hospital."

****

A Manchester couple discovered the wife was pregnant, but the family simply couldn't afford any more children. They looked around and found an excellent Hispanic family to adopt the child. Then...they found out she was going to have twins. Fortunately, a family of Arab immigrants agreed to adopt the other child. Twin healthy boys were born and passed on to the families, who named them Juan and Amal. The biological parents kept in close touch with the adoptive parents in a very amicable relationship. One day, Juan's family sent a picture of the youth in his cricket uniform. The biological mother was so proud of her son. She said to her husband: "He is so handsome. I wish we had a picture like this of our other son, too." He replied, "Dear, they are twins. When you've seen Juan, you've seen Amal."

****

There is a businessman who is not feeling well, so he goes to see the doctor about it. The doctor says to him: "Well, it must be your diet, what sort of greens do you eat?" The man replies: "Well, actually, I only eat peas, I hate all other green foods." The doctor is quite shocked at this and says: "Well man, that's your problem, all those peas will be clogging up your system, you'll have to give them up." The guy says, "But how long for? I mean I really like peas." The doctor replies, "For ever, I'm afraid." The man is quite shocked by this, but he gives it a go and sure enough, his condition improves, so he realizes that he will never eat a pea again. Anyway, one night, years later, he's at a convention for his employer and getting quite sloshed. One of the reps says: "Well, ashully, I'd love a cigarette, coz I avn't ad a smoke in four years, I gave it up." Quite a shocker really, and the barman goes: "Really? I haven't had a game of golf in three years, because it cost me my first marriage, so I gave it up." The businessman says, "Thas nuvving, I haven't ad a pea in six years." The barman jumps up screaming, "Okay, everyone who can't swim, grab a table..."

****

There was a country doctor who was the only doctor for miles around. He wanted to go on a fishing trip so he called the vet and asked him to look after things while he was gone. The vet asked: "Is anything happening?" The doctor replied, "Mrs Jones is about due, but I don't think the baby will come before I get back. Anyway, if it does, just deliver it. This is her third and the first two went really easily." The vet said: Okay", and the doctor went on the fishing trip. When he returned, he called the vet. "How did things go while I was gone?" "Pretty good." "Did Mrs Jones have her baby?" "Yes, it was a 8 pound boy. Everyone's doing fine." "Did you have any trouble?" "Well, there was just one little problem." "What was that?" "I had a terrible time getting her to eat the afterbirth."

****

A man and a woman were waiting at the hospital donation centre. Man: "What are you doing here today?" Woman: "Oh, I'm here to donate some blood. They're going to give me £5 for it." Man: "Hmm, that's interesting. I'm here to donate sperm, myself. But they pay me £25." The woman looked thoughtful for a moment and they chatted some more before going their separate ways. Several months later, the same man and woman met again in the donation centre. Man: "Oh, hi there. Here to donate blood again?" Woman: [shaking her head with mouth closed] "Unh unh."

****

Max Brown, a young father-to-be, was waiting anxiously outside the maternity ward where his wife was giving birth to their first baby. As he paced the floor, a nurse popped her head around the door. "It's a boy, Mr Brown," she said, "but we think you'd better go and have a cup of coffee because there might be another." Max turned a little pale and left. Some time later, he rang the hospital and was told he was the father of twins. "But," the nurse went on, "we're sure there's another on the way. Ring back again in a little while." At that, Max decided that coffee was not nearly strong enough. He ordered a few beers and rang the hospital again, only to be told a third baby had arrived and a fourth was imminent. White-faced, he stumbled to the bar and ordered a double scotch. Twenty minutes later, he tried the phone again, but he was in such a state that he dialled the wrong number and got the recorded cricket score. When they picked him up off the floor of the phone box, the recording was still going strong, "the score is 96 all out, and the last one was a duck."

****

A therapist told a woman to use some imagination while making love with her husband to spice things up. She replied, "You mean imagine that it's good?"

****

Patient: "Doc, Doc, if I give up wine, women, and song, will I live longer?" Doctor: "Not really. It will just seem that way."

****

A group of psychiatrists go to tour an insane asylum that is known for it's progressive rehabilitation methods. They begin by visiting some of the patients. The first patient they visit is a young woman. She is practising ballet. One of the psychiatrists asks: "What are you doing?" She replies, "I'm studying ballet so when I get out of here I can possibly join a troupe and be a productive member of society." "Wow, that's wonderful." The next person is a man reading a book with a pile of books next to him. The same question is asked of him, "What are you doing?" "I'm studying biology, chemistry, and physics, so I can enter medical school when I get out." Room after room, they witness the incredible success and attitudes of the patients. Until they finally reach a room the asylum's director is reluctant to open. Finally, he is persuaded to open it. Inside is a man balancing a peanut on his penis. The psychiatrist exclaims, "My God what are you doing?" The man replied: "I'm fucking nuts and I'm never getting out of here."

****

Doctor: "What seems to be the trouble? " Patient: "Doctor, I keep getting the feeling that nobody can hear what I say." Doctor: "What seems to be the trouble?"

****

Patient: "My tongue tingles when I touch it to a cracked walnut wrapped in used toaster-oven aluminium foil, what's wrong with me?" Doctor: "You have far too much free time."

Patient: "How much to have this tooth pulled?" Dentist: "£90." Patient: "£90 for just a few minutes work?" Dentist: "I can extract it very slowly if you like."

****

There was once a guy whose tongue was so long that when he stuck it out for the doctor, the nurse went, "Aaaaaahhh!"

****

Mrs Smith: "Help me, doctor! Little Tommy's swallowed the can-opener." Doctor: "Don't panic. He'll be alright." Mrs Smith: "But how do I open the frigging beans, the toast's getting cold."

****

A woman goes to the dentist. As he leans over to begin working on her, she grabs his balls. The dentist says: "Madam, I believe you've got a hold of my privates." The woman replies, "Yes. We're going to be careful not to hurt each other, aren't we."

****

A man, 92 years old, is told by his doctor that he has tested positive for HIV. Distraught and befuddled, he retires as usual to spend the afternoon at the park bench with other senior citizens. He tells his friend: “Can you believe it? I have HIV...at 92.” His friend replies, “You think you have troubles? I have IBM at 80.”

****

A woman goes to the hospital to visit a girlfriend who is about to have a heart transplant. She’s worried about the friend so she speaks to the doctor. Girlfriend: “I’m worried about my friend doctor. What if her body rejects the organ?” Doctor: “Well, she’s 36 years old and healthy. How long has she been in business?” Girlfriend: “She’s been working since she was 19 years old but what does that have to do with anything?” Doctor: “Well, she’s been working 17 years and hasn’t rejected an organ yet.”

****

This guy took his nymphomaniac wife to the sex therapist for treatment. “This is one hot potato of a lady, doctor,” he said, “maybe you can do something for her? She goes for any man, any age, any time, any where...and it is just driving me crazy with jealousy.” “We’ll see,” the therapist said. He directed the wife into his examining room, closed the door behind her, and told her to get undressed. Then he told her to get up on to the examining table on her stomach. The moment he touched her buttocks, she began to squirm and moan. It was too much for him to resist, so he climbed up on top of her and began screwing her. The husband heard the moans and groans coming from the examination room and, very suspicious, burst into the room. He was confronted by the sight of the doctor astride his wife and banging away. "Doctor, what are you doing?" he asked. Flustered, the therapist replied, "Oh, it's you. I'm only taking your wife's temperature." The husband pulled out a large pocket knife and began to hone it deliberately on his boot. "Well, doctor," he said, "when you take that thing out, it had better have numbers on it."

****

An old man of 87 went to the hospital to get a radical new surgical procedure done where they stretch the skin and pull all the wrinkles up on to the top of the scalp making you appear years younger. On his way out of the hospital, he met an old friend who didn't recognize him at first. "Rob, is that really you?" said the friend. "You look years younger. I didn't know you had a dimple in your chin." "It's not a dimple, it's my belly button" said the old man and his friend laughed. "If you think that's funny, take a look at what I'm wearing for a tie."

****

Patient: "I am having a hard time hearing. I cannot even hear myself cough." Doctor: "Here is a prescription, take the medicine for seven days, then return for a check-up." Seven days later – Patient: "Thanks a million, doctor. At least, I can hear myself cough NOW. So what did you do to make me hear better?" Doctor: "Not much, I gave you an expectorant to increase your cough."

****

A woman walks into her sex therapist's office. She tells the therapist that her husband is not a very good lover, and they never have sex any more, and she asks what to do about it. The therapist tells her that there is an experimental drug that might do the trick. She tells the woman to give her husband one pill that night and come back in the morning and tell her what happens. The next day, the woman comes in ecstatic, telling the therapist that the pill worked and that she and her husband had the best sex ever. She asks her therapist what would happen if she gave her husband two pills and the therapist says she doesn't know, but to go ahead and try it. The next day, the same thing happens, the woman comes in telling the therapist that the sex was even better than the night before and what would happen if she gave him five pills. The therapist says she doesn't know, but to go ahead and try it. The next day, the woman comes in limp but happy, and tells the therapist that the sex just keeps getting better and what would happen if she gave her husband the rest of the bottle. The therapist says she doesn't know; it's an experimental drug and she doesn't know what a full bottle could do to a person. Anyway, the woman leaves the therapist's office and puts the rest of the bottle of pills in her husband's morning coffee. A week later, a boy walks into the therapist's office and says: "Are you the dick-head who gave my mother a bottle of experimental pills?" "Why, yes, young man, I did. Why?" "Well, Mum's dead, my sister's pregnant, my arse hurts, and Dad's sitting in the corner going 'Here, kitty, kitty, kitty'..."

****

Patient: "Will it hurt, doctor?" Doctor: "Only when you get my bill."

****

After making love, the woman said to the man: "So, you're a doctor?" "That's right," replied the doctor smugly. "Bet you don't know what kind of doctor." "Ummm...I'd say that you're an anaesthetist." "Yes, that's right. Good guess. How did you know?" asked the man. "Because throughout the entire procedure, I didn't feel a thing."

****

A friend of mine went to the dentist recently. He commented that it must be tough spending all day with your hands in someone's mouth. He said, "I just think of it as having my hands in their wallet."

****

One day, a man walked into the dentist's office for some dental work. The dentist said: "Sir, you have a tooth I must pull, What type of painkiller would you like?" The man looked at the dentist and said, "None, thanks, I have experienced the second greatest pain in my life." The dentist said, "Sir, pulling this tooth will be painful, I suggest a painkiller." The man looked back at the dentist and said, "I have experienced the second greatest pain in my life. Nothing else will ever compare." The dentist said, "Sir, I'm telling you, use a painkiller." The man again said to the dentist, "I have experienced the second greatest pain in my life, I do not need painkillers, now pull the tooth." The dentist then said, "Okay, you asked for it, but first, tell me what was the second greatest pain in your life?" The man said, "Yes, I remember it well. I was hunting in some woods north of here one snowy day. Walking through the woods, the urge came upon me and I headed over to a tree. Well, I started to do my thing, and when the first part dropped, it set off a large bear trap that was hidden in the snow that closed on my balls. That was the second greatest pain in my life." The dentist then said, "Ouch! But then what was the first greatest pain in your life?" The man replied, "When I reached the end of the chain."

****

Three nurses died and went to the Pearly Gates. St Peter asked the first one: "What did you do on Earth that you deserve to get in here? The first nurse replied, "I was an intensive care nurse and I saved hundreds of lives." "Welcome," said St Peter, "come right in. And what did you do?" he asked the second one. The second nurse replied,

"I was an emergency room nurse and I saved hundreds of lives." "Welcome," said St Peter, "come right in. And what did you do?" he asked the third one. The third nurse replied, "I was a managed care nurse and I saved the taxpayer hundreds of thousands of pounds." "Welcome," said St Peter, "come right in... but only for three days."

****

A patient goes to a psychiatrist. The psychiatrist gives him a Rorschach Test; he shows a patient a circle with a dot inside it and asks, "What do you see?" The patient replies, "Two people are having sex in the middle of the circular room." The psychiatrist shows the patient another picture of a square with a dot inside it and asks, "What do you see?" Patient answers, "Two people are having sex in the square room." The psychiatrist shows the patient one more picture of a triangle with a dot outside it and asks: "What do you see now?" Patient replies, "What are you, some kind of pervert?"

****

"Oh doctor," moaned the woman to the psychiatrist. "Everyone calls me a nymphomaniac." "I understand," said the doctor, "but I'll be able to take better notes if you'll let go of my penis."

****

Patient: "Doc, Doc, I keep thinking that I'm a deck of cards." Psychiatrist: "Sit over there and I'll deal with you later."

****

Doctor: "Did you take the patient's temperature?" Nurse: "No. Is it missing?"

****

It is said that the limbic system of the brain controls the four Fs: Feeding, Fighting, Fleeing, and Reproduction.

****

Patient: "Doc, Doc I think I swallowed a pillow." Doctor: "How do you feel?" Patient: "A little down in the mouth."

****

Patient: "Doc, Doc, I can't stop stealing things." Psychiatrist: "Take these pills. They should help you." Patient: "But what if they don't?" Psychiatrist: "Then get me a video."

****

A city doctor started a practice in the countryside. He once had to go to a farm to attend to a sick farmer who lived there. After a few housecalls he stopped coming to the farm. The puzzled farmer finally phoned him to ask what the matter was. The doctor said, "it's your ducks at the entrance... Every time I enter the farm, they insult me."

****

Gynaecologists have a power that makes some men envious. They can go into a room where a woman is waiting for them and say, "Get undressed. I'll be with you in a minute."

****

After her operation, the famous lady soap-opera star was propped up in bed in her private room, as the doctor did his rounds. "Tell me, how are you feeling now?" he asked. "A lot better, thank you," purred the star in reply. "But one thing does bother me. When will I be able to resume a normal sex life?" "Oh, that's rather hard to say," said the doctor, "I've never been asked that after a tonsillectomy before."

****

A man swallowed a mouse while sleeping on the couch one day. His wife quickly called the doctor and said: "Doc, Doc, please come quickly. My husband just swallowed a mouse and he's gagging and thrashing about." "I'll be right over," the doctor said. "In the meantime, keep waving a piece of cheese over his mouth to try to attract the mouse up and out of there." When the doctor arrived, he saw the wife waving a piece of smoked herring over her husband's mouth. "Er, I told you to use cheese, not herring, to lure the mouse." "I know, doctor," she replied, "but first I've got to get the bloody cat out of him."

****

Man: "Doc, Doc, my wife thinks she's a refrigerator." Psychiatrist: "Don't worry, it will pass." Man: "But, doctor, when she sleeps with her mouth open, the damn light keeps me awake."

****

"Congratulations, Mr Brown, you're in great shape for a man of sixty. Pity you're only forty."

****

Patient: "Tell me, doctor. Is it serious?" Doctor: "Well, I wouldn't advise you to start reading any thick books."

****

Hypnotist: "Alright, Mr Henry, when I say wake up you will no longer be shy but full of confidence and be able to speak your mind... Wake Up." Patient: "Right, you! How about giving me a refund, you money-grabbing old quack."

****

A woman has just started to play golf when she gets stung on the arm by a bee. She rushes back to the clubhouse, hoping to find a doctor. She asks: "Is anyone here a doctor?" One fairly drunk guy stands up and says: "I'm a doctor, what can I help you with?" "I've been stung by a bee." "Oh really, where?" "Between the first and second hole" "Well, clearly your stance is too wide..."

****

A man speaks frantically into the phone, "My wife is pregnant, and her contractions are only two minutes apart." "Is this her first child?" the doctor queries. "No, you idiot!" the man shouts. "This is her husband."

****

A chap walks into a local pharmacy and walks up to the counter where a lady pharmacist is filling prescriptions. When she finally gets around to helping him he says, "I'd like 99 condoms please." With a surprised look on her face the pharmacist says, “You want 99 condoms! Fuck me!” To which the guy replies, “Make it 100.”

****

Doctor: “We need to get these people to a hospital.” Nurse: “What is it?” Doctor: “It’s a big building with a lot of doctors in it. Why do you ask?”

****

Patient: “Doc, Doc, I’ve got five penises.” Doctor: “Well, how do your pants fit?” Patient: “Like a glove.”

****

Patient walks into a doctor’s office. Patient: “Doc, Doc, people ignore me.” Doctor: “Next.”

****

Patient: “Doctor, doctor. My hair keeps falling out. What can you give me to keep it in?” Doctor: “A shoebox.”

****

A psychiatrist, who was just starting out, advertised his clinic as follows: "Satisfaction guaranteed or your mania back."

****

"Doctor, I don't understand what's going on with me. It's really strange, sometimes I feel like a teepee." The doctor thinks about it for a while and then urges the man to continue. So, the man continues, "and sometimes I feel like a wigwam." To which the doctor says: "I wouldn't worry about it, Fred, you're just two tents."

****

A man walked into a psychiatrist's office, sat down and took out a pack of cigarettes. He removed a cigarette from the pack, unrolled it, and stuffed the tobacco up his nose. The shrink frowned and said, "I see you need my help." The guy said, "Yeah doctor. Got a match?"

****

A man goes to the doctor's office one day. The attractive nurse says: "The doctor is over at the hospital right now. He won't be back for about an hour. Could you tell me your symptoms, please?" He tells her. She looks at him appraisingly and decides he's just tense. She offers: "Well, um, for £50, I've got just the thing for you." He agrees, and she takes him into an examining room and screws the daylights out of him. About a week later, he returns, only to find that the doctor is there. The doctor listens to the man's symptoms, examines him, and decides the man is just tense. The doctor writes out a prescription for a sedative and says, "That'll be £150 for this visit." The man says, "If it's all the same to you, doctor, I'd rather have the £50 cure."

****

As the doctor completed an examination of the patient, he said: "I can't find a cause for your complaint. Frankly, I think it's due to drinking." "In that case," said the patient, "I'll come back when you're sober."

****

The brash young gynaecologist, fresh out of medical school, took one look at his voluptuous new patient and abandoned his professional ethics entirely. As he stroked the supple skin of her naked body, he asked: "Do you understand what I am doing?" "Yes," the patient answered. "You're checking for dermatological abrasions." "Correct," the doctor lied. Next, he fondled her breasts long and lovingly. Again, he inquired, "do you understand what I am doing?" "You're feeling for cancerous lumps," she ventured. "Very astute," the doctor complimented, getting more excited. He placed the woman's feet in stirrups, dropped his pants, and slipped his member inside her. "And do you know what I am doing now?" "Yes, you're catching herpes."

Patient: "Doc, Doc, I think I need glasses." Teller: "You certainly do. This is a bank."

****

Patient: "Doc, Doc, should I file my nails?" Doctor: "No, throw them away like everybody else."

****

Mavis: "My daughter believes in preventative medicine, doctor." Doctor: "Oh, really?" Mavis: "Yes, she tries to prevent me from making her take it."

****

Have you heard about the new medication that is both an aphrodisiac and a laxative? It's called "Easy Come, Easy Go."

****

Patient: "Doc, Doc, you must help me. I'm under such a lot of stress, I keep losing my temper with people." Doctor: "Tell me about your problem." Patient: "I just did, you stupid bastard."

****

Bill: "Doc, Doc. My wife beats me." Doctor: "Oh dear. How often?" Bill: "Every time we play Scrabble."

****

"The doctor said he would have me on my feet in two weeks." "And did he?" "Yes, I had to sell the car to pay the bill."

****

Woman: "Doc, Doc, my husband tells me my pussy's too big. So I'd like you to tell me if you find it unusual." Doctor: "Please, take off your clothes and I'll examine you. [shouting] What a giant pussy. What a giant pussy." Woman [angry]: "Did you have to say it twice?" Doctor: "I didn't."

****

Patient: "Doc, Doc, when I wasn't married, I had six abortions, and now I've got married and can't get pregnant." Doctor: "Evidently you don't breed in captivity."

****

First man: "There's a guy who lives up the street from me who used to work in construction. One day last year his hand got run over by a bulldozer. Whatever those doctors did, it's really amazing – today he's a concert pianist." Second man: "That's nothing. I knew a guy in college – laziest bum I ever knew. He was really fat and out of shape. He was trying to hitch a ride one day and got hit by a truck. Broke nearly every damn bone in his body. Somehow they put him back together better than he was before. Now he's a triathlete and he's planning to try out for the Olympics." Third man "Yeah, well I knew this poor retarded kid. He couldn't do a whole lot, but someone at the dynamite factory got charitable and gave him a job as a stockboy. He was working in the warehouse one day and got locked in. It was dark and he couldn't find the door. Not being too bright, he lit a match to try to find his way. The whole place exploded. All they could find of him was a few fingers and his eyebrows. From that little bit they were able to put him back together and today that kid is the president of the USA."

****

Doctor: "You're in good health. You'll live to be 80." Patient: "But, doctor, I am 80 right now." Doctor: "See, what did I tell you?"

****

A child psychologist for a school is asked to see a pupil who draws all his pictures with black and brown crayons. He talks to him. Nothing obvious. He gives him projective tests. Nothing shows up. Finally, in desperation, he gives him some paper and a box of crayons. "Oh goody," says the boy, "I got an old box in school and only black and brown were left."

****

One night in the pub, the Landlord is lamenting the fact that business is so quiet on Mondays, Tuesdays and Wednesdays. As he moans to some of the regulars a stranger, dressed in a tweed jacket and wearing glasses wanders over and says: "I'm sorry, but I couldn't help overhearing your conversation. I'm a doctor at the lunatic asylum up the road and I'm trying to integrate some of the more sane individuals into the community. Why don't I bring some of my patients along, say next Tuesday. You'll have some customers and my patients will have a night out." Well, the publican isn't sure but the thought of more paying customers on a quiet night appeals, so he agrees. So, the following Tuesday the guy in the tweed jacket and glasses shows up with about ten lunatics. He says to the publican: "Give them whatever they want, let them practise paying with milk bottle tops, put it on a tab and I'll settle up at closing time." The publican has a great time selling loads of drinks and encouraging the loonies to eat crisps and peanuts. The loonies have a great time, getting drunk but they behave themselves and hand over bottle-top money for their drinks. At closing time the publican adds up the bill and it comes to just over a hundred pounds. The guy with the glasses and the tweed jacket starts to organize the loonies ready to take them back to the asylum. Finally he comes over and asks for the bill. The publican, feeling that he's charged them rather a lot and feeling he should do his bit to help these poor unfortunate people gives him a discount. "It's 80 quid," he says. The guy in the tweed jacket smiles and says: "That's fine. Have you got change for a dustbin lid?"

****

A man working at a lumberyard is pushing a tree through a bandsaw when he accidentally shears off all his fingers and thumbs. He rushes to the emergency entrance of a nearby hospital where the awaiting doctor takes a look and says. "Yuck! Well, give me the fingers and I'll see what I can do." "I haven't got the fingers." The doctor says, "What do you mean, you haven't got the fingers? This is the age of medical advances. We've got microsurgery and all sorts of incredible techniques. Why didn't you bring me the fingers?" "Well, heck, doctor. I tried, but I couldn't pick 'em up."

****

The patient shook his doctor's hand in gratitude and said: "Since we are the best of friends, I would not want to insult you by offering payment. But I would like you to know that I have mentioned you in my will." "That is very kind of you," said the doctor emotionally, and then added, "Can I see that prescription I just gave you? I'd like to make a little change..."

How do you tell which nurse is the head nurse? The one with scuffed knees.

****

A proctologist is the rare profession in which the doctor starts out at the bottom and stays there.

****

The crofter's wife went into labour in the middle of the night, and the doctor was called out to assist in the delivery. To keep the father-to-be busy, the doctor handed him a lantern and said: "Here, you hold this high so I can see what I'm doing." Soon, a lusty baby boy was brought into the world. "Och!" said the doctor. "Don't be in a rush to put the lantern by...I think there's yet another wee bairn to come." Sure enough, within minutes he had delivered a bonnie lass. "Na, dinna be in a great hurry to be putting down that lantern, lad...It seems there's yet another one besides," cried the doctor. The crofter scratched his head in bewilderment, and asked the doctor: "Well, now, mon. Do ye suppose the light's attracting them?"

****

Patient: "Doc, Doc, I keep thinking I'm a curtain." Psychiatrist: "Pull yourself together."

Patient: "Doc, Doc, I keep thinking I'm invisible." Psychiatrist: "Who said that?"

****

Patient: "Doc, Doc, I keep thinking I'm a dustbin." Psychiatrist: "Don't talk such rubbish."

****

Patient: "Doc, Doc, I keep thinking I'm a billiard ball." Psychiatrist: "Get to the end of the queue."

****

Patient: "Doc, Doc, my wife thinks I'm crazy because I like sausages." Psychiatrist: "Nonsense! I like sausages too." Patient: "Good, you should come see my collection. I've got hundreds."

****

Patient: "Doc, Doc, people tell me I'm a wheelbarrow." Psychiatrist: "Don't let them push you around."

****

Doctor: "Did you take those pills I gave you to improve your memory?" Patient: "Pills?"

****

I was 12 years old before I realized I could cough without having a doctor holding my bollocks.

****

A somewhat advanced society has figured how to package basic knowledge in pill form. A student, needing some learning, goes to the pharmacy and asks what kind of knowledge pills are available. The pharmacist says: "Here's a pill for English literature." The student takes the pill and swallows it and has new knowledge about English literature. "What else do you have?" asks the student. "Well, I have pills for art history, biology, and world history," replies the pharmacist. The student asks for these, and swallows them and has new knowledge about those subjects. Then the student asks: "Do you have a pill for maths?" The pharmacist says, "Wait just a moment," goes back into the storeroom, brings back a whopper of a pill, and plonks it on the counter. "I have to take that huge pill for maths?" inquires the student. The pharmacist replied, "Well, you know maths always was a little hard to swallow."

****

A pipe burst in a doctor's house. He called a plumber. The plumber arrived, unpacked his tools, did mysterious plumber-type things for a while, and handed the doctor a bill for £600. The doctor exclaimed: "This is ridiculous. I don't even make that much as a doctor." The plumber waited for him to finish and quietly said: "Neither did I when I was a doctor."

****

A man is having problems with his dick which certainly has seen better times. He consults a doctor who, after a couple of tests, says: "Sorry, but you've overdone it the last 30 years, your dick is burned out. You won't be able to make love more than 30 times." The man walks home deeply depressed; his wife is already expecting him at the front door and asks him what the doctor said concerning his problem. He tells her what the doctor told him. She says: "Oh my god, only 30 times. We should not waste that; we should make a list." He replies, "Yes, I already made a list on the way home. Sorry your name is not on it."

****

A Jewish boy was walking with his girlfriend in the grounds of his father's house. His father was a successful doctor, and was carrying out a circumcision in the on-site surgery. As they were walking, they heard a scream and a foreskin flew out of the window and landed at the girl's feet. "What's this," she asked. "Taste it," he replied, "If you like it, I'll give you a whole one."

****

Wife: "Doc, Doc, my husband thinks he's a horse." Psychiatrist: "He is just probably a little stressed out and needs some rest." Wife: "But he kicks chairs and eats grass and doesn't even sleep in the bed." Psychiatrist: "Well, in that case, it looks like he may need a lot of help, but it may cost quite a lot of money for prolonged treatment." Wife: "Oh you don't have to worry about the money part. Last Sunday, he won the Grand National."

****

"I'm worried," said the woman to her sex therapist. "I happened to find my daughter and the boy next door both naked and examining each other's bodies." "That's not unusual," smiled the therapist. "I wouldn't worry about it." "But I am worried, doctor," insisted the woman, "and so is my son-in-law."

****

Patient: "Doc, Doc, you've got to help me. Every time I sneeze, I have an orgasm." Doctor: "Really! What are you taking for it?" Patient: "Black pepper."

Patient: "Doc, Doc, you've got to help me. I eat apples, apples later come out into the toilet. I eat bananas, bananas come out." Doctor: "That's easy. Eat shit."

****

Patient: "Doc, Doc, you've got to help me. Every night I get the uncontrollable urge to go downstairs and stick my dick into the biscuit tin. Do you know what's wrong with me?" Doctor: "Yes... You're fucking crackers."

****

What do puppies and near-sighted gynaecologists have in common? They both have wet noses.

****

Patient: "Doc, Doc, I have yellow teeth, what do I do?" Dentist: "Wear a brown tie..."

****

There are two businessmen, whose names happen to be Mr Turtle and Mr Carrot and, one day, as they were coming back from lunch, Mr Turtle says to Mr Carrot: "You know, you're getting fat." To which Mr

Carrot says, "You're not so slim yourself." So Mr Turtle says, "Okay, we'll see who is the least fit, race you back to the office." So the race starts and they have only got about a hundred yards down the street when Mr Turtle crosses the road in front of a car and gets knocked down. Mr Carrot sees that he's in a pretty bad way, so he rushes to the phone and calls Mr Cabbage, the ambulance driver. Mr Cabbage duly arrives and piles Mr Turtle into the ambulance and rushes to a hospital. Mr Turtle follows and as soon as he gets to the hospital he asks the nurse, Miss Cauliflower, whether he will be alright. "Miss Cauliflower, Miss Cauliflower, will Mr Turtle be alright?" She replies, "Well, I couldn't really say, you'll have to ask Dr Bean." So he rushes over to Dr Bean and says, "Dr Bean, Dr Bean, will Mr Turtle be alright?" And the doctor says, "Well, I wouldn't like to say, you'd best ask the specialist, Dr Pea." So of course, Mr Carrot rushes over to Dr Pea and says, "Dr Pea, Dr Pea, will Mr Turtle be alright?" And Doctor Pea says, "I've done all I can for him, it's all in the hands of the Surgeon, Dr Turnip." So Mr Carrot waits outside the surgery for three hours until they have finished the operation and rushes up to Dr Turnip and says, "Dr Turnip, Dr Turnip, will Mr Turtle be alright?" Dr Turnip turns to him and says, "We did all we could, but I'm afraid he'll be a vegetable for the rest of his life..."

****

Once I was sick and I had to go to an ear, nose, and throat specialist. There are ear doctors, nose doctors, throat doctors, gynaecologists, proctologists. Any place you have a hole, there's a guy who specializes in your hole. They make an entire career out of that hole. And if the ear doctor, nose doctor, throat doctor, gynaecologist, or proctologist can't help you, he sends you to a surgeon. Why? So he can make a new hole.

****

What do you call a gynaecologist who specializes in geriatric care? A spreader of old wives' tails.

****

A proctologist pulls out a thermometer from his shirt pocket. He looks at it and says: "Shit, some arsehole has my pen."

****

What is the proper medical term for the circumcision of a rabbit? A hare cut.

****

A guy hasn't been feeling well for a while, so he goes to the doctor for a check-up. After he sees the doctor, the doctor tells him he has a very serious condition and says that he would like to talk to the man's wife. So the man leaves and sends his wife in. The doctor tells the wife that her husband has a very serious condition and that he is going to die. However, the doctor tells her that there is one way she can save his life – she must cook him three meals a day and have sex with him every night for six months and then he'll be okay. When the wife leaves the office her husband asks her what the doctor said. She looks at her husband and tells him: "He said you're gonna die."

****

This guy goes to the doctor for a vasectomy. Unlike the usual patients, he shows up in a Rolls Royce, and sits in the doctor's office in a tuxedo with black tie. The doctor says, "I've done a lot of these, but I've never seen a Rolls and tuxedo before. What's the story?" To which the fellow responds, "If I'm gonna BE impotent, I'm going to LOOK impotent."

****

A man is talking to the family doctor. "Doctor, I think my wife's going deaf." The doctor answers, "Well, here's something you can try on her to test her hearing. Stand some distance away from her and ask her a question. If she doesn't answer, move a little closer and ask again. Keep repeating this until she answers. Then you'll be able to tell just how hard of hearing she really is." The man goes home and tries it out. He walks in the door and says: "Honey, what's for dinner?" He doesn't hear an answer, so he moves closer to her. "Honey, what's for dinner?" Still no answer. He repeats this several times, until he's standing just a few feet away from her. Finally, she answers: "For the eleventh time, I said we're having MEATLOAF."

****

An elderly woman went into the doctor's office. When the doctor asked why she was there, she replied: "I'd like to have some birth control pills." Taken aback, the doctor thought for a minute and then said, "Excuse me, Mrs Smith, but you're 75 years old. What possible use could you have for birth control pills?" The woman responded, "They help me sleep better." The doctor thought some more and continued, "How in the world do birth control pills help you to sleep?" The woman said: "I put them in my granddaughter's orange juice and I sleep better at night."

****

Patient: "What's good for excessive wind, doctor?" Doctor: "A kite."

****

A woman went to her new doctor for a check-up. He turned out to be absolutely gorgeous. He told her he was going to put his hand on her back and he wanted her to say "eighty-eight." "Eighty-eight," she purred. "Good. Now I'm going to put my hand on your throat and I want you to again say 'eighty-eight.'" "Eighhty...eighhhhtttt." "Fine. Now I'm going to put my hand on your chest and I want you one more time to say 'eighty-eight.'" "One, two, three, four, five..."

****

A man goes to see his doctor. He pokes himself in the arm, leg, and torso, complaining that it hurts when he does this. The doctor asks him if he is Irish. The man replies that he is. To which the doctor replies that the man's finger is broken.

****

An extremely old man visits his doctor and tells him, "I need my sex drive lowered." The doctor, incredulous, says, "What? You want your sex drive lowered?" To which the old man replies: "It's all in my head; I need it LOWERED."

****

Doctor: "Does it hurt when you do this?" Patient: "Yes." Doctor: "Well, don't do it, then."

****

Patient: "Doc, Doc what should I do if my temperature goes up a point or more?" Doctor: "Sell!"

****

After much soul searching and having determined the husband was infertile, the childless couple decided to try artificial insemination. When the woman showed up at the clinic, she was told to undress from the waist down, get on the table and place her feet in the stirrups. She was feeling rather awkward about the entire procedure when the doctor came in. Her anxiety was not diminished by the sight of him pulling down his pants. "Wait a minute. What the hell is going on here?" yelled the woman, pulling herself into a sitting position. "Don't you want to get pregnant?" asked the doctor. "Well, yes, I do," answered the woman. "Then lie back and spread 'em," replied the doctor. "We're all out of the bottled stuff. You'll just have to settle for what's on tap."

****

Dentist: "Could you help me? Could you give me a few of your loudest, most agonised screams?" Patient: "Why? It isn't that bad." Dentist: "Well, there are loads of people in the waiting room, and I'm playing golf at four."

****

Did you hear about the two blood corpuscles named Romeo and Juliet? They loved in vein.

****

Three doctors are in the duck blind and a bird flies overhead. The GP looks at it and says: "Looks like a duck, flies like a duck...it's probably a duck," and shoots at it, but he misses and the bird flies away. The next bird flies overhead and the pathologist looks at it, then looks through the pages of a bird manual, and says: "Hmmmm...green wings, yellow bill, quacking sound...might be a duck." He raises his gun to shoot it, but the bird is long gone. A third bird flies over. The surgeon raises his gun and shoots almost without looking, brings the bird down, and turns to the pathologist and says: "Go and see if that was a duck, would you old chap?"

****

Doctor: "Have you ever had this before?" Patient: "Yes." Doctor: "Well, you've got it again."

****

A woman starts dating a doctor. Before too long, she becomes pregnant and they don't know what to do. About nine months later, just about the time she is going to give birth, a priest goes into the hospital for a prostate gland infection. The doctor says to the woman: "I know what we'll do. After I've operated on the priest, I'll give the baby to him and tell him it was a miracle." "Do you think it will work?" she asks the doctor. "It's worth a try," he says. So the doctor delivers the baby and then operates on the priest. After the operation he goes in to the priest and says, "Father, you're not going to believe this." "What?" says the priest. "What happened?" "You gave birth to a child." "But that's impossible." "I just did the operation," insists the doctor. "It's a miracle! Here's your baby." About 15 years go by, and the priest realizes that he must tell his son the truth. One day he sits the boy down and says, "Son, I have something to tell you. I'm not your father." The son says, "What do you mean, you're not my father?" The priest replies, "I'm your mother. The archbishop is your father."

****

The new mother got out of bed for the first time since giving birth, dressed in her robe and walked down the hospital hallway to the nurse's desk where she asked for a phone book. "What are you doing out here? You should be in your room resting," the nurse exclaimed. "I want to search through the phone book for a name for my baby," the new mother replied. "You don't have to do that here. The hospital furnishes a booklet to all new mothers to assist them in picking a first name for their baby." "You don't understand," the woman said and frowned, "my baby already has a first name."

A man comes to a doctor because of sore throat. The doctor tells him to pull down his pants and to swing his genitals out of the window. "What does this have to do with my throat?" "Nothing, I just hate the neighbours."

****

A sex therapist was doing research at the local college when one of the male volunteers told him: "When I get it in part way, my vision blurs. And when I get it all the way in, I can't see a thing." "Hmmm...that's an interesting optical reaction to sex," said the researcher. "Would you mind if I had a look at it?" So the volunteer stuck out his tongue.

****

The head doctors in a lunatic asylum have a meeting and decide that one of their patients is potentially well. So they decide to test him and take him to the movies. When they get to the movie theatre, there are 'wet paint' signs pointing to the benches. The doctors just sit down, but the patient puts a newspaper down first and then sits down. The doctors get all excited because they think he may be in touch with reality now. So they ask him: "Why did you put the newspaper down first?" He answers: "So I'd be higher and have a better view."

****

Guys & Dolls

4

Jokes about Men, Women and Relationships

Choose a wife by your ear rather than by your eye.

****

Take an interest in your husband's activities: hire a detective.

****

Sex is hereditary. If your parents never had it, chances are you won't either.

****

Never try to guess your wife's size. Just buy her anything marked 'petite' and hold on to the receipt.

****

Insurance is like marriage. You pay, pay, pay, and you never get anything back.

****

Don't marry for money; you can borrow it cheaper.

****

Husband: "Darling, will you love me when I'm old and feeble?"
Wife: "Of course I do, Honey."

****

Sex is like snow; you never know how many inches you are going to get or how long it is going to last.

****

Irritated wife: "What do you mean by coming home half drunk?"
Hubby: "It's not my fault...I ran out of money."

****

Think how much fun you could have with the doctor's wife and a bucket of apples.

****

Brains x Beauty x Availability = 1

****

It is always the wrong time of the month.

Sex is a three-letter word which needs some old-fashioned four-letter words to convey its full meaning.

****

What do men and women have in common? They both distrust men.

****

Women who love only women may have a good point.

****

Bachelors know more about women than married men; if they didn't, they'd be married too.

****

How does an older woman keep her youth? By giving him money.

****

Never argue with a woman when she's tired...or when she's rested.

****

A lady is a woman who never shows her underwear unintentionally.

****

Why did God give woman nipples? To make suckers out of men.

****

Never hit a man with glasses. Hit him with a baseball bat.

****

Women! You can't live with them, you can't do most positions without them.

****

Men are those creatures with two legs and eight hands.

****

A woman was chatting with her next-door neighbour. "I feel really good today. I started out this morning with an act of unselfish generosity. I gave a fiver to a dosser." "You mean you gave a dosser five quid? That's a lot of money to give away like that. What did your husband say about it?" "He said 'Thanks'."

If only women came with pull-down menus and online help...

****

Women! You can't live with them, and you can't get them to dress up in a skimpy Nazi costume and beat you with a warm courgette.

****

Why are men endowed with a half ounce more brains than dogs? So they know not to embarrass themselves by humping women's knees at parties.

****

A young couple met with their priest to set a date for their wedding. When he asked whether they preferred a contemporary or a traditional service, they opted for the contemporary. On the big day, a major storm forced the groom to take an alternate route to the church. The streets were flooded, so he rolled up his trouser legs to keep them dry. When he finally reached the church, his best man rushed him into the sanctuary and up to the altar, just as the ceremony was starting. "Pull down your trousers," whispered the priest "Er, Reverend, I've changed my mind," the groom responded. "I think I want the traditional service."

My opinions are my wife's, and she says I'm damn lucky to have them.

****

Whenever a husband and wife begin to discuss their marriage, they are giving evidence at an inquest.

****

A husband and his wife advertised for a live-in maid to cook and do the housework. A likely-looking girl came in from the country, and they hired her. She worked out well, was a good cook, was polite, and kept the house neat. One day, after about six months, she came in and said she would have to quit. "But why?" asked the disappointed wife. She hummed and hahed and said she didn't want to say, but the wife was persistent, so finally she said: "Well, on my day off a couple of months ago I met this good-looking fellow from over in the next county, and well, I'm pregnant." The wife said: "Look, we don't want to lose you. My husband and I don't have any children, and we'll adopt your baby if you will stay." She talked to her husband; he agreed, and the maid said she would stay. The baby came, they adopted it, and all went well. After several months though, the maid came in again and said that she would have to quit. The wife questioned her, found out that she was pregnant again, talked to her husband, and offered to adopt the baby if she would stay. She agreed, had the baby, they adopted it, and life went on as usual. In a few months, however, she again said she would have to leave. Same thing – she was pregnant. They made the same offer, she agreed, and they adopted the third baby. She worked for a week or two, but then said, "I am definitely leaving this time." "Don't tell me you're pregnant again?" asked the lady of the house. "No," she said, "there are just too many damn kids here to tidy up after."

****

It doesn't much signify who one marries, for one is sure to find out next morning it was someone else.

****

Marriage: A ceremony in which rings are put on the finger of the lady and through the nose of the gentleman.

****

How can you tell which bottle contains the PMT medicine? It's the one with bite marks on the cap.

****

A man and woman were on their honeymoon after a long and very happy courtship. On their honeymoon, they decide to take their horses through the beautiful mountain passes of Europe. The horses are crossing a small stream when the woman's horse stumbles and jostles the man's wife. Once across the stream, the man dismounts, walks over to the horse and stares into its eyes. Finally, he states: "That's one." The man remounts his horse and they continue their ride. A bit further down the path, the woman's horse stumbles when stepping over a fallen tree. The man dismounts, stares the horse in the eyes, and boldly states: "That's Two!" He returns to his saddle and they move on. As the afternoon sun began to set, the woman's horse loses its footing on a mossy slope. The man dismounts, moves to the woman's horse, and helps his wife out of the saddle. The man, moving to the front of the horse, stares it in the eyes and firmly says: "That's three." He removes a pistol from his coat, and shoots the horse dead. The woman, quite upset at seeing the beautiful horse killed, says to her husband, "That's terrible, why would you do such a thing." The man stares at his wife and firmly says: "That's one!"

****

If you meet somebody who tells you that he loves you more than anybody in the whole wide world, don't trust him; it means he experiments.

****

If a man hears what a woman says, she is not beautiful.

During the wedding ceremony, when the minister comes to the part about, "If anyone knows any reason why these two people should not marry, speak up now or forever hold your peace," have a four-year-old boy run up the aisle yelling, "Daddy, Daddy..."

****

Why do men snore? When they fall asleep, their balls cover their arseholes and they get blow-back.

****

Besides "I love you", what three words does a wife want to hear most? "I'll fix it."

****

In olden times, sacrifices were made at the altar, a practice which is still very much practised.

****

If the effort that went in to research on the female bosom had gone into the space program, we would now be running hot-dog stands on the moon.

A woman may very well form a friendship with a man, but for this to endure, it must be assisted by a little physical antipathy.

****

If one man can wash one stack of dishes in one hour, how many stacks of dishes can four men wash in four hours? None. They'll all sit down together and watch football on television.

****

In marriage, as in war, it is permitted to take every advantage of the enemy.

****

No man should marry until he has studied anatomy and dissected at least one woman.

****

A man and woman were lying in bed one night and the woman said to the man: "I really wish I had bigger tits." The man responded by saying she should rub toilet paper all over them. The woman looked at him and asked: "Toilet paper, what will that do?" The man said, "I don't know, but look what it's done for your arse."

Why are some men uncircumcised? The doctors were afraid of causing brain damage to the infant.

****

How are men like UFOs? You don't know where they come from, what their mission is, or what time they're going to take off.

****

What is a wedding tragedy? To marry a man for love, and then find out he has no money.

****

What's the best thing to come out of a penis? The wrinkles.

****

Most men prefer looks to brains, because most men see better than they think.

****

It destroys one's nerves to be amiable every day to the same human being.

Adam was created first to give him a chance to say something.

****

"I'd like my wife to be beautiful, well-behaved, smart and rich," the bachelor said. "Oh, well," his friend replied, "then you have to get married four times."

****

Women! If you want to know why they are called the 'opposite sex', express an opinion.

****

A woman was complaining to her best friend over lunch. "Every time my husband climaxes, he lets out an ear-splitting yell." "That doesn't sound all that bad to me," said her friend. "As a matter of fact, that would kind of turn me on." "It would me too," said the first woman, "if it didn't keep waking me up."

****

Where do you have to go to find a man who is truly into commitment? A mental hospital.

The newlywed wife said to her husband when he returned from work: "I have great news for you. Pretty soon, we're going to be three in this house instead of two. The husband glowed with happiness and kissed his wife until she added: "I'm glad that you feel this way, as tomorrow morning my mother moves in with us."

****

What's the best way to have your husband remember your anniversary? Get married on his birthday.

****

It now costs more to amuse a child than it once did to educate his father.

****

A man was complaining to a friend: "I had it all – money, a beautiful house, a big car, the love of a beautiful woman; then, Pow! it was all gone." "What happened?" asked the friend. "My wife found out..."

****

"We have a terrible time making ends meet on Bob's income," his wife told her best friend. "How do you two manage? And you even have kids." "We get along okay," her friend said, "you see, we work on our budget every evening. That saves us lots of money." "Really? How can that be?" "Well, by the time we get it all balanced, it's too damn late to go anywhere and do anything."

****

No matter how many times you've had it, if it's offered, take it, because it'll never be quite the same again.

****

What could men do to make their marriages last longer? Pay less attention to prenuptial agreements and more to postnuptual affection and sex.

****

A beggar walks up to a well-dressed woman who is shopping in Knightsbridge and says: "I haven't eaten anything in four days." She looks at him and says: "God, I wish I had your willpower."

****

Most husbands don't like to hear their wives struggling with housework; so they turn up the volume on the television.

Two bits of advice to the new bride: 1) tell your new husband that you have to have one night a week out with the girls, and 2) don't waste that night with the girls.

****

"It's just too hot to wear clothes today," said Jack as he stepped out of the shower. "Honey, what do you think the neighbours would think if I mowed the lawn like this?" "That I married you for your money."

****

What is the only time a man thinks about a candlelight dinner? When the power goes off.

****

What do most men think mutual orgasm is? An insurance company.

****

What is the one thing that all men at singles bars have in common? They're married.

****

Behind every great man, there is a surprised woman.

****

Three honeymoon couples find themselves in adjacent rooms in a hotel. As they are getting undressed, the first man says to his wife: "What huge buttocks." Much offended, she threw him into the corridor. The second man, also undressing, says to his wife: "Christ! What huge tits." She is also greatly offended and throws him out into the corridor. Several minutes later, the third newlywed husband arrives in the corridor as well. The other two ask: "What happened? Did you put your foot in it?" "No, but I could have," the third man replied.

****

Why do women change their minds so often? To keep them clean.

****

Why is it never the cold girl who gets given the fur coat?

****

Fred and Jane were relating their holiday experiences to a friend. "It sounds as if you had a great time in Cornwall," the friend observed, "but didn't you tell me you were going to Scotland?" "Yes, it's just ridiculous," said Jane, "Fred simply will not ask for directions."

****

Why do women rub their eyes when they wake up in the morning? Because they don't have any balls to scratch.

****

Why do men name their penises? Because they don't like the idea of having a stranger make 90 per cent of their decisions.

****

Do it only with the best.

****

Don't keep him in the doghouse too often or he might give his bone to the woman next door.

****

Love is an ideal thing, marriage is a real thing. A confusion of the real with the ideal never goes unpunished.

Did you hear about the scientist whose wife had twins? He baptized one and kept the other as a control.

****

Women are one of the Almighty's enigmas, created to prove to men that He knows more than they do.

****

What matters is not the length of the wand, but the magic in the stick.

****

Have you heard about the couple who got married in a nudist colony? They wanted everyone to be sure who the best man was.

****

If life were fair, the acquisition of a large bosom or a massive inheritance would have no bearing on your ability to attract the opposite sex.

****

Love is the delusion that one man or woman differs from another.

Marriage is a ceremony that turns your dreamboat into a barge.

****

I told my wife that a husband is like a fine wine; he gets better with age. The next day, she locked me in the cellar.

****

The bachelor who complained that the women he selected would not remain his friend for more than a few weeks, was told: "Your problem is that you are looking for a particular kind of woman. You ought to be looking for the kind of woman who is not particular."

****

Every mother generally hopes that her daughter will snag a better husband than she managed to do...but she's certain that her boy will never get as great a wife as his father did.

****

A recent survey shows that the commonest form of marriage proposal these days consists of the words: "You're WHAT?"

****

When do men insist that women are illogical? When a woman doesn't agree with them.

****

Marriage has driven more than one man to sex.

****

Women truly are better than men. Otherwise, they'd be intolerable.

****

Why is food better than men? Because you don't have to wait an hour for seconds.

****

I don't worry about terrorism. I was married for two years.

****

How can a woman tell if she is having a super orgasm? Her husband wakes up.

****

A person receives a telegram informing him of his mother-in-law's death. It also enquires whether the lady should be buried or burnt. He replies: "Don't take chances. Burn the body and bury the ashes."

****

Bachelors should be heavily taxed. It is not fair that some men should be happier than others.

****

The definition of a husband: A man who stands by his wife in troubles she'd never have been in if she hadn't married him.

****

Why are men and spray paint alike? One squeeze and they're all over you.

****

"I'd like to buy some gloves for my wife," the young man said, eyeing the attractive salesgirl, "but I don't know her size." "Will this help?" she asked sweetly, placing her hand in his. "Oh, yes," he answered. "Her hands are just slightly smaller that yours." "Will there be anything else?" the salesgirl queried as she wrapped the gloves. "Now that you mention it," he replied, "she also needs a bra and knickers."

****

Seems that my latest Freudian slip came just as my wife arrived back from a week-long business trip. As she grabbed her luggage and headed off, she asked, "Did you miss me?" I replied quite innocently, "It's been so hard without you."

****

Why don't men often show their true feelings? Because they don't have true feelings.

****

A best man's speech should be like a mini-skirt – short enough to be interesting, but long enough to cover the bare essentials.

****

Watching her mother as she tried on her new mink coat, the daughter protested, "Mum, do you realize some poor, dumb beast suffered so you could have that coat?" Her mother glared back at her and said, "Don't talk about your father that way."

My wife has a split personality, and I hate both of them.

****

The three different stages of sex in marriage: tri-weekly; try weekly; try weakly.

****

Two men who hadn't seen each other in years met on the street. While they were talking and trying to catch up on all those intervening years, one asked the other if he had got married. "No," the other man replied. "I look this way because someone just spilled a cup of coffee on me."

****

Marriage is the high sea for which no compass has yet been invented.

****

If you want to sacrifice the admiration of many men for the criticism of one, go ahead, get married.

****

Marriage is a three-ring circus: engagement ring, wedding ring and suffering.

****

Being a woman is quite difficult since it consists mainly of dealing with men.

****

A husband is living proof that a wife can take a joke.

****

Why are men like popcorn? They satisfy you, but only for a little while.

****

Men always want to please women, but these last 15 years women have been hard to please. If you want to resist the feminist movement, the simple way to do it is to give them what they want and they'll defeat themselves. Today, you've got endless women in their twenties and thirties who don't know if they want to be a mother, have lunch, or be Secretary of State.

Marry not a tennis player. For love means nothing to them.

****

A truck stops to pick up a female hitchhiker. The driver opens the door and says: "Come on in. I'm not like the other ones that only let the good-looking girls have a ride."

****

Marriage is a rest period between romances.

****

Why is being a penis not all its cracked up to be? Because you have a head, but no brains. There's always a couple of nuts following you around. Your neighbour's an arsehole and your best friend's a cunt.

****

Fidelity is a virtue peculiar to those who are about to be betrayed.

****

Why are men like paper cups? They're disposable.

Hot dogs come in packs of ten, buns in packs of eight, beer in packs of six, ham comes in packs of 16 slices, condoms come in packs of three. Why can't they get it straight? Nowadays, a man needs a calculator just to have a weekend...

****

When the lights are out, all women are beautiful.

****

They say that men only think about sex. That's not exactly true. They also care a lot about power, world domination, money, and beer.

****

A successful man is one who makes more money than his wife can spend. A successful woman is one who can find such a man.

****

An ideal wife is one who remains faithful to you but tries to be just as charming as if she weren't.

****

One night, while a woman and her husband were making love, she suddenly noticed something sticking in his ear. When she asked him what it was he replied: "Be quiet, woman. I'm listening to the cricket."

****

I was engaged myself once. To a contortionist. But she broke it off.

****

Sow your wild oats on Saturday night – then on Sunday, pray for crop failure.

****

A young couple were on their honeymoon. The husband was sitting in the bathroom on the edge of the bathtub saying to himself, "Now how can I tell my wife that I've got really smelly feet and that my socks absolutely stink? I've managed to keep it from her while we were dating, but she's bound to find out sooner or later that my feet stink. Now how do I tell her?" Meanwhile, the wife was sitting in the bed saying to herself, "Now how do I tell my husband that I've got really bad breath? I've been very lucky to keep it from him while we were courting, but as soon as he's lived with me for a week, he's bound to find out. Now how do I tell him gently?" The husband finally plucked up enough courage to tell his wife and so he walked into the bedroom. He walked over to the bed, climbed over to his wife, put his arm around her neck, moveed his face very close to hers and said, "Darling, I've a confession to make." And she said, "So have I, love." To which he replied, "Don't tell me, you've eaten my socks."

****

Love: a temporary insanity often curable by marriage.

****

Women sometimes make fools of men, but most guys are the DIY type.

****

Love is the triumph of imagination over intelligence.

****

The doctor came out of the operating room to talk with the man's wife. "I don't like the look of your husband," he said. "Neither do I," said the wife, "but he's not home much, and he's great with the kids."

****

What's a man's idea of helping with the housework? Lifting his legs so you can vacuum.

****

Marriage is the process of finding out what kind of person your spouse would have really preferred.

****

The next door neighbour of a middle-aged wife came over to inform her that her retired husband was chasing around after young prostitutes. The woman smiled. "So what?" The neighbour was surprised, "It doesn't bother you that he's running around with those women?" The woman replied, "I have a dog who chases cars and buses, too."

****

Being a woman is of special interest to aspiring male transsexuals. To actual women it is simply a good excuse not to play football.

****

There are five types of sex involved in a marriage. The first is Smurf Sex. This happens during the honeymoon; you both keep doing it until you're blue in the face. The second is Kitchen Sex. This is at the beginning of the marriage; you'll have sex anywhere, anytime. Hence, also in the kitchen. The third kind is Bedroom Sex. You've calmed down a bit, perhaps have kids, so you have to do it in the bedroom. The fourth kind is Hallway Sex. This is where you pass each other in the hallway and say: "Fuck you!" The fifth kind is Courtroom Sex. This is when you get divorced and your wife fucks you in front of everyone in court.

****

On the first evening of their honeymoon, they were sitting on the balcony of the hotel while the sun was setting. "Honey," she said, "now that we're married, will you tell me what a penis is?" He almost fell off the chair. Being her husband, he led her into their room and took his pants off. "This, my love, is a penis," he told her. "Oh!" she exclaimed, "it looks like a cock, only smaller."

****

A psychiatrist visited a Norwich mental institution and asked a patient, "How did you get here? What was the nature of your illness?" He got this reply... "Well, it all started when I got married and I reckon I should never have done it. I married a widow with a grown daughter who then became my stepdaughter. My dad came to visit us, fell in love with my lovely stepdaughter, then married her. And so my stepdaughter was now my stepmother. Soon, my wife had a son who was, of course, my daddy's brother-in-law, since he is the half-brother of my stepdaughter, who is now, of course, my daddy's wife. So, as I told you, when my stepdaughter married my daddy, she was at once my stepmother. Now, since my new son is brother to my stepmother, he also became my uncle. As you know, my wife is my step-grandmother since she is my stepmother's mother. Don't forget that my stepmother is my stepdaughter. Remember, too, that I am my wife's grandson. But hold on just a few minutes more. You see, since I'm married to my step-grandmother, I am not only the wife's grandson and her hubby, but I am also my own grandfather. Now can you understand how I got put in this place?"

****

How are men like noodles? They're always in hot water, they lack taste, and they need dough.

****

My mother-in-law broke up my marriage. My wife came home from work one day and found me in bed with her.

****

Nothing astonishes men so much as common sense and plain dealing.

Why are women so much more interesting to men than men are to women?

****

One good turn gets most of the duvet.

****

A man needs a mistress, just to break the monogamy.

****

Love is a thousand miles long, but comes in six-inch instalments.

****

Sometimes I wonder if men and women really suit each other. Perhaps they should live next door and just visit now and then.

****

I've sometimes thought of marrying, and then I've thought again.

****

A woman was getting married. She entered the church wearing a black wedding gown that surprised everyone. The pastor was a bit annoyed and asked her: "Why are you dressed up in black?" The woman replied: "Well, that's because I'm not a virgin."

****

When a woman gets married, she wants the three S's: Sensitivity; Sincerity; and Sharing. What does she get? The three B's: Belching; Body odour; and Bad breath.

****

You know you've been married too long when a "quickie" before dinner now means a drink.

****

It's sad that a married couple can be torn apart by something as simple as a pack of wild dogs.

****

It's not true that married men live longer than single men. It only seems longer.

A young couple get married and they've never made love before. On their wedding night, the new bride is quite anxious to get things going, but the man seems to be having some difficulty. Finally, he starts to undress. When he takes off his pants, she notices that his knees are deeply pockmarked and scarred. So his wife says, "What happened to you?" The man says, "When I was young, I had the kneesles." He then takes off his socks and his wife sees that his toes are all mangled and deformed. "Hmmm, well what happened to your feet?" inquires the wife. "When I was a young boy, I had tolio." So, finally, the man takes off his shorts and the woman says: "Don't tell me. Smallcox, right?"

****

This guy is getting married and he is a bit nervous since he is not too experienced. So he asks his best man to come along on the honeymoon and give a few pointers. The best man exclaims, "Come on man, its your honeymoon, you're supposed to be spending time with your wife, not your best friend." To which the groom replies that he has already paid for a room next door to his for the best man. After much coercion, the best man give in and decides to go along. They work out a system where the best man will pound on the wall and shout advice if he hears anything going wrong. So the honeymoon arrives, and the bride and groom go to the honeymoon suite of the hotel, and the best man goes to his room next door. After a few moments, the bride gets undressed, but the groom gets so nervous he runs into the bathroom and locks the door. After about five minutes of waiting, the bride says, "Honey, are you coming out, I have to go to the bathroom." The groom replies, "I will be out in a few minutes, Hon, I'll be ready soon." After a few more minutes, the bride can't take it any longer, so she rummages under the bed where all the wedding gifts are stashed, grabs a box, unwraps it, pulls out the fondue pot, shits in it, wipes with the tissue paper, closes it and shoves it under the bed. Just then the groom, having summoned his manly nerve walks out of the bathroom. The bride, being feminine and all, goes into the bathroom to stall for a few minutes so the groom won't know what she did. The groom, sitting on the bed notices this awful smell. What can that be? He looks under the bed, finds the box, pulls it out and exclaims: "Honey, there's shit in your box." Boom! Boom! Boom! (There's pounding on the wall...) The best man yells from the other room, "Turn her over, turn her over."

****

Six months into a marriage, a man was asked by his best friend how everything was going. He replied: "Oh, just fine. We practically never have any arguments. In the morning, she does what she wants. In the afternoon, I do what she wants. And at night, we both do what we both want."

****

The days just before marriage are like a snappy introduction to a tedious book.

****

Anybody who claims that marriage is a 50/50 proposition doesn't know the first thing about women or fractions.

****

One cardinal rule of marriage should never be forgotten: "Give little, give seldom, and above all, give grudgingly." Otherwise, what could have been a proper marriage could become an orgy of sexual lust.

****

Ever notice how so many of women's problems can be traced to the male gender? MENstruation, MENopause, MENtal breakdown, GUYnaecology, HIMmorrhoids...

****

What happens when a man tries to hide his baldness by combing his hair across his head? The truth comes shining through.

****

The Great White Telephone to God

5

Jokes about Religion

“A Swedish bishop was getting ready to visit America. Some of his close associates advised him to be careful when responding to reporters on his arrival in New York. The bishop however was overconfident and paid little heed to the advice. During a press conference, held on his arrival at JFK airport, one reporter asked the bishop if he was planning on visiting any night clubs in New York. The bishop replied “Are there any night clubs in New York?” suggesting that he was ignorant of anything like night clubs in New York. To his surprise, the next morning’s papers had the following banner headlines: “While still on tarmac at JFK, Swedish Bishop asks, ‘Are there any night clubs in New York?’”

****

Two brothers went to confession; the younger one went in first. The priest always liked to ask questions of the children before their confession, so the priest asked the little boy: “Do you know where God is?” The little boy ran out and told his brother, “Let’s get the hell out of here, the priest has lost God and wants to blame it on me.”

****

A rabbi went to heaven and met God for the first time. A thought hit him and he asked God about what souls eat when they go to hell. God told him to look at what was being served. So the rabbi peeked down below the clouds and, behold, it was mealtime in hell. The souls there were being offered a seven-course meal with steak, mashed potatoes, tossed salad and a blue cheese sauce, and a bottle of wine was being passed round. Meanwhile God informed the rabbi that it was time for his meal – a peanut butter sandwich. The rabbi asked God why the guys down there were getting the royal treatment while he had to eat sandwiches. God replied: "It simply does not pay to cook for two."

****

A "Nuncio", where they exist, has the rank of an ambassador. While in Paris, Roncalli once said: "You know, it's rough being a Papal Nuncio. I get invited to these diplomatic parties where everyone stands around with a small plate of canapés trying not to look bored. Then, in walks a shapely woman in a low-cut, revealing gown, and everyone in the whole place turns around and looks – AT ME."

****

A man in the Middle Ages became fed up with humanity and decided to spend the rest of his life in a monastery. The abbot warned him that he would have to take a vow of silence and live the rest of his life as a scribe, to which the man replied, "No problem. I'm sick of talking." Ten years went by, and the abbot called for the man. He told him that he was a model monk and perfect scribe, and that they were very happy to have him. As per their tradition, he was allowed to say two words. Asked if he had anything to say, the man nodded and said:

"Food cold." The abbot sent him on his way. Ten years later, he was brought before the abbot again and once again told how pleased they were with his performance, and that he was again allowed two more words if he so chose. The man said: "Bed hard," and was sent back to work. Another ten years went by and again the abbot sent for the man, telling him that he was the best monk they had ever had, and that he was allowed another two words. The man nodded and said: "I quit." To this, the abbot replied in a disgusted tone: "Doesn't surprise me. You've done nothing but whinge since you got here."

****

A busload of priests have an accident and all of them are killed instantly. On arriving at the Pearly Gates, they find there's a terrible queue. St Peter is there looking at a big book, jotting down notes, mumbling occasionally. There is a person standing in front of his desk being processed. After some time St Peter says "Next" and another person steps up. The wait seems to take forever and there are an enormous number of people waiting, but St Peter doesn't seem to be hurrying. People are arriving all the time, some in mangled states, some famished and some looking "normal". Then a dishevelled man comes in, cigarette butt hanging from his lips like it has taken root. The stubble on his chin looks as though it could sand diamonds. He stands at the back of the queue like everyone else. St Peter however spies him and hurries over to him. "Oh come in, come in. Welcome! No need to queue, we have you already processed. Your residence is in order. There's special treatment for you." The priests have something to say about that. "Hey" says their spokesman, "how come he gets the special treatment? We are, after all, men of God." "That man," says St Peter, "was a taxi driver. He has scared the hell out of far more people than any of you lot."

****

A catholic priest felt despondent about being posted to a very rural parish in the middle of a forest. He wrote letters to his bishop constantly, requesting that he be posted somewhere more hospitable. No reply to his letters ever came and soon the letters stopped. Some time later, when the archbishop was making the rounds of the rural churches, he dropped in to see how the unhappy priest was doing. He found a pleasant man, in an air-conditioned church. There were no parishioners, since the closest neighbours were many miles away. The archbishop admitted to some confusion, since the priest did not look like the desperate writer of so many letters. He asked the priest how he liked it out in the woods. "At first I was unhappy. But thanks to two things I have grown to love it out here." "And they are?" the archbishop inquired. "The first is my Rosary. Without my Rosary I wouldn't make it a day out here." "And the second?" At this the priest looked askance. "Well, to be honest, I have developed a taste for Martinis in the afternoon. They help to alleviate the boredom during the worst part of the day." He looked sheepish at this admission, but the archbishop just smiled. "Martinis, eh? Well, that's not so bad. In fact, I'd be glad to share one with you right now, if you don't mind that is." "Not at all!" the priest exulted. "Let me get one for you right away." Turning to the back of the church, the priest shouted, "Oh, Rosie?... Marti?"

****

Why were most of Jesus' apostles fishermen and not cabinet makers? If they were cabinet makers, Jesus would have had to say: "Drop your drawers and follow me."

****

A group of new arrivals were sitting in the foyer in heaven, waiting for their turn to see St Peter. On the walls of the reception room were hundreds of clocks all ticking away. Every once in a while, however, a clock would suddenly move ahead several minutes in one jump. Curious, one fellow who was waiting turned to the receptionist and said: "Excuse me, but why do some of those clocks jump ahead now and then?" The receptionist answered: "Oh, those are the clocks that keep track of the days that people still have to live on Earth. Each person has a clock. Every time they do something sneaky or bad, they lose some of their allotted time on Earth and their clock jumps ahead a few minutes." Interested, the man asked, "Can I see my little daughter's clock?" "Sure, said the receptionist," and showed him a clock that ticked calmly and steadily along. "Now, can I see my wife's clock, please?" asked the man. "Why not?" said the receptionist and showed him a clock that for the most part ran smoothly, once in a great while jumping ahead two or three minutes at once. The man said, "You know, I was a Democrat back there on Earth, can I see Bill Clinton's clock?" "I'm afraid not," said the receptionist. "It's down in the accounting department. Their air conditioning broke this morning and they're using it for an electric fan."

****

Who is the most elastic man in the Bible? Balaam. He tied his ass to a tree and walked two miles into town.

****

A woman is nearly caught with her lover when her husband comes home early. To hide the man, she puts him in the closet, but the lover soon discovers that he is not alone. The breathing he hears belongs to the woman's young son. "Gosh, it's dark in here," says the boy. "Bloody hell, child, please shut up," replies the nervous man. "Well, mister, I think I'm going to scream." "Please, kid, don't scream." "Can I have some money?" asks the boy. "Well, here, here's five quid, it's all I've got." The boy, sensing that the man was lying, presses on. "I really feel like screaming." "No, kid, look, here's 50 quid, just don't scream." "Well, I don't know." "Here's the last of my money, just don't scream." The boy, satisfied, agrees to be quiet. Later, he went with his mother to a store where a brand new bike was on sale. When he tries to buy it with his new-found cash, his mother became suspicious of the source of this money. So, being a good catholic, she takes him to see the local priest in confession. "Gosh," says the boy, not used to being in the confessional, "it's dark in here." "Don't start with that again," says the priest.

****

Who is the most constipated man in the Bible? David – on the throne for 40 years.

****

How can you make God laugh? Tell Him your plans for the future.

****

A pious man lived right next door to an atheist. While the religious one prayed day in, day out, and was constantly on his knees in communion with his Lord, the atheist never even looked twice at a church. However, the atheist's life was good; he had a well-paying job and a beautiful wife, and his children were healthy and good-natured. The pious man's job was strenuous and his wages were low, his wife was getting fatter every day and his children wouldn't give him the time of day. So one day, deep in prayer as usual, he raised his eyes towards heaven and asked: "Oh God, I honour you every day, I ask your advice for every problem and confess to you my every sin. Yet my neighbour, who doesn't even believe in you and certainly never prays, seems blessed with every happiness, while I go poor and suffer many an indignity. Why is this?" And a great voice was heard from above: "BECAUSE HE DOESN'T BOTHER ME ALL THE TIME!"

****

A catholic, a jew, and an episcopalian are lined up at the Pearly Gates. The catholic asks to get in and St Peter says, "No, sorry." "Why not?" says the catholic, "I've been good." "Well, you ate meat on a Friday in Lent, so I can't let you in." The jew walks up and again St Peter says no. The jew wants an explanation so St Peter replies, "There was that time you ate pork...sorry, you have to go to the other place." Then the Episcopalian goes up and asks to be let in and St Peter again says no. "Why not?" asks the Episcopalian, "What did I do wrong?" "Well," says St Peter, "you once ate your *entrée* with the salad fork."

****

A man who is an avid golfer finally gets a once-in-a-lifetime chance for an audience with the Pope. After standing in line for hours, he gets to the Pope and says, "Holiness, I have a question that only you can answer. You see, I love golf, and I feel a real need to know if there is a golf course in heaven. Can you tell me if there is?" The Pope considers for a moment, and says, "I do not know the answer to your question, my son, but I will talk to God and get back to you." The next day, the man is called for another audience with the Pope to receive the answer to his question. He stands before the Pope, who says, "My son, I have some good news and some bad news in relation to your question. The good news is that heaven has the most fabulous golf course that you could imagine and is in eternally perfect shape. It puts all courses on Earth to shame. The bad news is that you tee-off tomorrow morning."

****

One sunny Sunday in spring, Father Fitzpatrick noticed that there was a smaller gathering than usual for the noon service. So as soon as the final hymn was sung, he slipped out the back way and went along the street to see who was out and about instead of coming to church. The first person he saw was old Mrs O'Neill, sitting on a park bench with her cane beside her. The good cleric sat down next to her and said, "Good afternoon, Mrs O'Neill, why weren't you in church today?" Mrs O'Neill replied: "Well, Father, it was just such a lovely day today I didn't want to be cooped up in that stuffy old church." The priest was a bit taken aback by this blunt answer, so he thought for a minute, then asked, "But Mrs O'Neill, don't you want to go to heaven?" To his surprise, the elderly lady shook her head vehemently and said, "No Father." At that, the priest got to his feet indignantly and said firmly, "Then I am ashamed for you." Now it was Mrs O'Neill's turn to be surprised. She looked up at him and said, "Oh, Father, I thought you meant right now."

****

The Pope was in the middle of an audience when his principal advisor whispered in his ear: "Your Holiness, I hate to interrupt, but the Messiah is on the phone and he wants to talk to you." The Pope excused himself so he could take the call in private. A few minutes later he came back out with a sombre expression. He said, "I have some good news and some bad news. The good news is that the call was from the Messiah, the Lord Jesus, our saviour, and the time of the second coming is at hand. The bad news is that he was calling from Salt Lake City."

****

A jew, a hindu and a baptist acquire a time machine. They decide that their first trip will be back to Bethlehem to witness the birth of Christ. They manage to arrive a little later than planned and find that there is only one room left at the inn and it has only one narrow bed. "It's perfectly alright," says the hindu, "material things are unimportant. I will go and sleep in the stable." He leaves, but ten minutes later there is a knock on the door. It is the hindu. "I'm sorry, but there is a cow in the stable. Cows are sacred and it would be quite improper for me to stay there." "Alright," says the jew, "you are, in a manner of speaking, my guests here. I will sleep in the stable." He leaves but ten minutes later there is a knock on the door. It is the jew,. "I'm sorry, I'm sorry, but there is a pig in the stable. I cannot possibly stay there." "Ah my friends," says the baptist, "was not our Lord Jesus unafraid to stay in poor lodgings of lowly estate? I will sleep in the stable," and he leaves. A few minutes later there is a knock on the door. It's the pig and the cow. The cow says: "Excuse me but there's a baptist in the stable..."

****

A jewish couple have a son who is a bit troublesome. At the age of five he starts in school, and pretty soon, his parents get to hear that things aren't going well. After a couple of months, they are asked to take him out of school, since he is not setting a good example to the other jewish children. Things go from bad to worse: after only a month in reform school he's thrown out again, and even the state correction centre can't deal with him. Eventually, in desperation, the parents take him to the only place left: a local catholic school. They don't hear anything concerning his performance, no reports of trouble, but their curiosity is really aroused when he comes home at the end of the term with a report card showing three "B"s and the rest "A"s. Things continue in the same vein, and at the end of the second term, he's running straight "A"s. By the end of the school year, his performance has been so good that he is top of the class. His mother takes him aside and asks, "What's going on? We send you to your own people, and they throw you out. The reform school can't deal with you, and even the state correction centre wasn't enough. But now, with these catholics, you're getting the best grades ever." "Well Mum," says the boy "I wasn't too bothered by those other places, but the first thing I see when I go into that catholic school is a jewish kid nailed to a couple of planks. I know when to back down."

****

Jesus returned and ended up by the side of the River Severn in Worcestershire. He confronted an old boy who was sat there fishing. "I am Jesus – I have come to save all from the horrors that be," exclaimed the great one. "Sod off, you're scaring the fish," answered the old one. "No, you don't understand – I have returned to save the Earth, now tell me, where should I start?" The old boy thinks for a while and tells him to perform a miracle, then he will believe that this is truly The Lord. "Walk across the river," he tells Jesus. So Jesus starts walking across the river, and the water is lapping round his ankles – then around his shins, then his knees. This starts worrying him, but he continues, knowing that he can do it. The next thing he knows, he slips and disappears under the water, and nearly drowns. He manages to claw his way back to the shore, and the old man says to him: "There you are, see, you're not Jesus, you can't walk across water." Jesus responds, "Well, I used to be able to do it until I got these nail holes in my feet."

What do you get when you cross a devil worshipper with a jehovah's witness? Someone who goes from door to door telling people to go to hell.

****

What do you get when you cross a Mafia soldier with a jehovah's witness? Lots of converts.

****

Who was the first computer operator in the Bible? Eve, she had an Apple in one hand and a Wang in the other.

****

A well-known politician dies and goes to heaven. At the Pearly Gates he is met by St Peter and led in. St Peter speaks: "Well, you committed a few teeny weenie sins while you were alive, didn't you? Lying is something we're a bit hot on at the moment, and, as a politician..." "Say no more," says the politician, "you've got me there." "Right then, since you did so much good generally for your country, we're prepared to let you in, but you'll have to do penance for two years. You will have to spend that time with this woman." At this, the most hideously deformed, smelly, gossiping woman appears. The politician appears to blanch slightly, but says: "Fair enough, I guess it's worth it for eternity in paradise." "Good man, this way now." St Peter leads them through a door into a vast chamber, filled with white-robed couples, chatting and laughing with each other. Sweet music and the aroma of rose blossom fill the air, and angels and cherubs flutter about. Suddenly, the politician notices his old rival, whose death had preceded his by a matter of weeks. Amazingly, this man is arm in arm with a beautiful model. "What the hell is this," storms the politician. "That man was the worst thing to happen to my country for 200 years. He destroyed everything I stood for, and was totally dishonest in doing it. How come I get two years with this hag, while he gets to cavort with a beautiful model?" "Steady on," says St Peter, "let me explain. That's not your rival doing his penance, it's the model doing hers."

****

There was an elderly Alabama widow who lived in a large mansion. She was feeling generous when it came to Thanksgiving, so she called up the local military base, and asked to speak with the lieutenant. "Please send up four nice young men to eat dinner here on Thanksgiving, but please, don't send any jews. Please, no jews." The lieutenant replied, "No problem ma'am, and I am sure I speak for the army when I say we all appreciate your kindness." Well, Thanksgiving rolled around, and the widow went to answer the door when the bell rang. She was surprised to see four of the blackest boys that anyone had ever seen, especially in the south. "But, but, there must be some mistake," she stammered. One of them replied: "No ma'am Lieutenant Goldstein doesn't make mistakes."

****

Two navvies were digging a ditch across from a brothel, and one noticed a rabbi walk into the place. One said to the other, "It's a sad day when men of the cloth walk into a place like that." After a little while, the other man saw a minister walk into the brothel. He stood up and said to his partner, "Did you see that? It's no wonder the children today are so confused with the example that the clergy are setting for them." After about another hour, the first man saw a catholic priest walk in. He promptly stood up and proclaimed to his partner. "Aye, that is truly sad. One of the poor lassies must be dying."

****

M sends James Bond on a secret mission to heaven. When M doesn't hear from Bond for over a day, he gets worried and calls up heaven. The Virgin Mary picks up the phone and says "Virgin Mary speaking." M asks her if Bond has reached there yet. She replies that he hasn't. M waits another few hours and calls heaven back again. "Virgin Mary speaking," comes the response. "Is James there yet?" asks M. Again the answer is no. M is really worried by this time but he waits for a few more hours and then calls heaven back again. "Hello, Mary speaking..."

Where in the Bible does it describe the most people in one automobile? In The Acts of the Apostles it says that 100 people went to Jerusalem “in one Accord”.

****

What’s the difference between Jesus and a picture of Jesus? It only takes one nail to hang up the picture.

****

St Peter was at his post at the Pearly Gates and in rather a bad mood. That day only couples were on line to get in. “Next,” he called out, in a bored fashion. Up stepped a couple. “Name?” asked St Peter. “Smith,” replied the husband. St Peter slowly looked up from his desk, looked them over for a moment, and finally asked with a bit of a sneer: “says here that you were a Banker in your time, Smith.” St Peter then leaned forward, pointed his finger at them, and said: “You know, I don’t like bankers. You’re cheap. Always grubbing for money...cheating people...I don’t know if I want to let you two in here today. So what’s your wife’s name?” “Penny,” replied Mr Smith. “PENNY!” exclaimed St Peter. “Look at that, you even married a woman named after money. Get out of here, try again some other time. Next,” he called out, still agitated. Up stepped the next couple. “Name?” asked St Peter. “Jones”, replied the husband. Again St Peter slowly looked up from his desk, looked them over for a moment, and asked with a sneer: "Jones the Publican?" "Why, yes," said Mr Jones. St Peter again leaned forward, pointing his finger at them, and said: "You know, I don't like publicans. You drink too much. Always getting drunk on your own stock and throwing up all over the streets...beating up your wives and kids during drunken rages...I don't know if I want to let you two in here today. So what's your wife's name?" "Sherri" replied Mr Jones. "SHERRI!" exclaimed St Peter. "Look at that, you even married a woman named after a drink. Get out of here, try again some other time." Meanwhile, several couples back, a man overhearing all of this turns to his wife and says: "Let's get out of here Fanny."

****

A man dies, and finds himself in heaven. St Peter offers to give him the tour. They walk around a little, and the man sees samoans worshipping God in a samoan way, and zoroastrians worshipping in a zoroastrian way, and Eskimos worshipping in an Eskimo way, and so on...on and on, till at one point they come to an enormous fortress made of stone, completely sealed off, with no windows or doors. Dimly, from within, they can hear the sound of wild partying. "Shhh," says St Peter. "Be very quiet." The two tiptoe past the fortress in utter silence, and when they have left it a way behind, the man turns to St Peter and says, "Why did we have to be so quiet back there? Who's in the fortress?" St Peter answers, "Oh, those are the jehovah's witnesses. They don't know anyone else is here."

A pastor was addressing the children during the Christmas service. "Who is the mother of Jesus?" he asked them. Without hesitation, dozens of tiny voices chorused back "Mary." "That's right. Now who can tell me who is the father of Jesus?" There was quiet and fidgeting. After all, no-one had told them there was going to be a quiz. Then a young girl spoke up. With assurance, she boldly announced: "I know. It's Virg." After two more seconds of silence the entire community erupted in laughter. Of course – we all know it was Virg an' Mary.

****

The pastor of a small congregation was trying to find a contractor to paint his church. Because the church fund was low and he couldn't pay very much, he selected the lowest bidder. The contractor decided to make the job pay better by skimping on materials. He thinned the paint with solvent and then only applied one coat. Within months, the poor paint job began to flake away and the church looked worse than it had before the work was done. The pastor sent a note to the contractor that said: "Repaint, repaint – thin no more!"

****

Jesus walked into a bar in Balham. He approached three sad-faced gentlemen at a table, and greeted the first one: "What's troubling you, brother?" he said. "My eyes. I keep getting stronger and stronger glasses, and I still can't see." Jesus touched the man, who ran outside to tell the world about his, now, 20-20 vision. The next gentleman couldn't hear Jesus' questions, so The Lord just touched his ears, restoring his hearing to perfection. This man, too, ran out the door, praising God. The third man leapt from his chair and backed up against the wall, even before Jesus could greet him. "Don't you come near me, man. Don't touch me!" he screamed. "I'm on disability benefits."

****

Did you hear about the child who thought Jesus was a giant teddy bear called Gladly, who had something wrong with his eyes, because every time she went to church they would sing "Gladly the cross I'd bear."

****

Blessed is he who expects no gratitude, for he shall not be disappointed.

****

A priest and a rabbi found themselves seated together on a long trans-Atlantic flight. They started talking and became quite friendly. The priest slyly said to the rabbi: "Tell me the truth rabbi. Have you ever tried a ham sandwich?" The rabbi confessed that he had once tried a ham sandwich. Then the rabbi asked the priest: "You chaps are supposed to be celibate. Have you ever had sex with a woman?" The priest confessed that he had. "Beats the hell out of a ham sandwich, doesn't it?" said the rabbi.

****

The man died. Having not lived an all-that-honest life he found himself at the gates of hell. "Welcome to hell" announced the Devil greeting him warmly. "Glad you could join us. As your last taste of free will, you are allowed to choose which of three possible places in which you will spend the rest of eternity." There were three doors behind the Devil. He opened the first door. Flames shot into the room and the man could see thousands of people in the fire. "No," said the man, "not this one." The Devil opened the second door. The man could see thousands of people slaving away at a large rock pile. They were all being whipped as they hammered the large boulders into smaller boulders. "No," said the man again. Finally, the Devil opened up that last door which showed thousands of people in an incredibly large lake with vomit up to their chins. All of them were chanting: "Don't make waves, don't make waves..." "That's awful!" commented the man in revulsion. "You think that's bad?" asked the Devil. "You should see it when the Angels spend the weekend here water-skiing."

****

Assorted crisps & snacks

6

Gags, One-liners, Limericks and other variations on Books, Mothers, Chickens, Seven-course Dinners and other strangenesses

Have you heard about the new book, *Care For Your Lawn*? It's by Ray King.

****

Have you heard about the new book, *Speeding Up Your Work*? It's by Sheik Aleg.

****

"Mum, Mum! What's a werewolf?" "Shut up and comb your face."

****

What's the difference between a cat and a bagel? You can put a bagel in the toaster, but you have to put the cat in the oven.

****

Have you heard about the new book, *Be a Winner*? It's by Vic Trees.

****

Have you heard about the new book, *The Day We Bunked Off*? It's by Marcus Absent.

There was an old girl of Kilkenny
Whose usual charge was a penny.
For half of that sum
You could finger her bum;
T'was a source of amusement for many.

****

Why did the graduate student cross the road? He was writing a dissertation on chickens.

****

Why did the second chicken cross the road? He was stapled to the first chicken.

****

There was a young lady from Kew
Who filled her vagina with glue.
She said with a grin,
"If they pay to get in,
They'll pay to get out of it too!"

****

Have you heard about the new book, *A Long Walk Home*? It's by Miss D Buss.

****

There was a young man of St John's
Who wanted to bugger the swans.
But the loyal hall porter
Said, "Pray take my daughter,
Those birds are reserved for the dons."

****

What is a politician's seven-course dinner? A piece of essential vote-winning employment for catering staff.

****

"Mum, Mum! Why is my hair so slimey?" "Shut up, you little snot."

****

Have you heard about the new book, *An African Trek*? It's by Dusty Rhodes.

****

Have you heard about the new book, *Saudi Arabian Transport*? It's by I Rhoda Camel.

****

How many country and western singers does it take to change a lightbulb? Four: one to change it; one to sing about how heartbroken he is at the loss of the old one; one to sing about how madly in love she is with the new one; and one to go "Yeeeee-Hah!" and throw his hat in the air.

****

Have you heard about the new book, *A Guide to Causing Chaos*? It's by Ken Fusion.

****

Have you heard about the new book, *A Guide to Japanese Fashion*? It's by Kimm Ono.

****

Have you heard Broadmoor's answering machine? It says: "Welcome to the Psychiatric Hotline. If you are obsessive-compulsive, please press 1 repeatedly. If you are co-dependent, please ask someone to press 2. If you have multiple personalities, please press 3, 4, 5 and 6. If you have paranoid delusions, we know who you are and what you want; just stay on the line until we can trace your call. If you are schizophrenic, listen carefully and a little voice will tell you which number to press. If you are depressed, it doesn't matter which number you press. No one will listen to your message."

****

Have you heard about the new book, *From Highwayman to Mugger*? It's by Andy Tover.

****

Have you heard about the new book, *Everyman's Guide To Emergency Repair*? It's by Jerry Rigg.

****

Have you heard about the new book, *A Guide To Basingstoke*? It's by Helen Earth.

****

How many jewish mothers-in-law does it take to change a lightbulb? None: they'll just sit in the dark, knowing full well you can't be bothered to do a simple thing like change a lightbulb for them, and after all they've done for you...

****

Do you know how many jazz musicians it takes to change a light bulb? No, but hum a few bars and I'll fake it.

****

Have you heard about the new book, *The Hero Through History*? It's by Ben Evolence.

****

A Scotsman who lived on the loch
Had holes down the length of his cock.
He could get an erection,
And play a selection
Of Johann Sebastian Bach.

****

Have you heard about the new book, *Give Him The Push*? It's by Eve Ho.

Have you heard about the new book, *No Bovver, the story of Hover*? It's by Lorne Moor.

****

There once was a man from Cape Horn
Who wished that he'd never been born.
He wouldn't have been
If his father had seen
That the end of his condom was torn.

****

Have you heard about the new book, *Locked In The Safe*? It's by Xavier Breath.

****

Why did the chicken cross the road? To show the hedgehog it was possible.

****

"Mum, Mum! Why are we pushing the car off the cliff?" "Shut up, you'll wake your father."

How many Seventies disco dancers does it take to change a lightbulb? Two: one to boogie up the ladder and one to say "Get daaoowwn!"

****

How many members of the royal family does it take to screw in a lightbulb? "Actually none. As your queen I would like to reassure the people of the Commonwealth that while our family may have had our Annus Horribilis and while some of us may have screwed in the stables or in the mud, none of us, to my knowledge, has actually screwed in a lightbulb."

****

There once was a man from Nantucket
Whose dick was so long he could suck it.
He said with a grin,
As he wiped off his chin,
"If my ear was a cunt, I would fuck it."

****

How many inner-city gang members does it take to screw in a lightbulb? Four: one to rob the off licence to get money for the bulb; one to drive the getaway car; one to screw it in; and one to hold his crack pipe while he does it.

Have you heard about the new book, *The Naughty Schoolboys*? It's by Tanya Hydes.

****

Have you heard the English Foundation's answering machine? It says: "This is the literacy self-test hotline. After the tone, leave your name and number, and recite a sentence using today's vocabulary word. Today's word is 'supercilious'."

****

Have you heard the disorganized girl's answering machine? It says: "Hello. I'm home right now but cannot find the phone. Please leave a message and I will call you back as soon as I find it."

****

Have you heard the mad scientist's answering machine? It says: "The machine answering this message is connected to a 5000 volt power supply and a relay, which is wired to this small kitten. (Sound of a kitten meowing). If you hang up before you leave a message, it will complete the circuit and fry the kitty. The choice is yours."

****

Have you heard the MI6 agent's answering machine? It says: "This is John's answering machine. Please leave your name and number, and after I've doctored the tape, your message will implicate you in a serious crime and be brought to the attention of Scotland Yard."

****

Have you heard the suicidal bloke's answering machine? It says: "Sorry, I'm far too depressed to come to the phone. If you can be bothered, leave a message after the sound of the gunshot, and maybe somebody will call you I guess..."

****

Have you heard the Psychic Hotline's answering machine? It says: "This is not an answering machine – this is a telepathic thought-recording device. After the tone, think about your name, your reason for calling, and a number where I can reach you, and I'll think about returning your call."

****

Have you heard about the new book, *The Fabrics Revolution*? It's by Polly Ester.

****

Have you heard about the new book, *The Population Problem in North-West France*? It's by Francis Crowded.

****

Have you heard about the new book, *Modern Business Practice*? It's by Hiram Cheep.

****

What's worse than finding a dead cat on your pillow in the morning? Realizing you were drunk and made love to it the night before.

****

What's pink and spits? A cat in a frying pan.

****

What is a Canadian seven-course dinner? A six pack of Molson and a moose.

****

What is a student's seven-course dinner? A six pack of Red Bull and a slice of pizza.

What is an American seven-course dinner? A six pack of Bud Lite and a Big Mac.

****

Have you heard about the new book, *Prepare Your Own Will*? It's by Paul Bearer.

****

How many antelopes does it take to change a lightbulb? None: They are herbivorous animals who live in a primarily grassland habitat and therefore have no need for artificial light sources.

****

What is a Scottish seven-course dinner? Six crumbs of stale bread and a case of whisky.

****

Have you heard about the new book, *Hymns for Our Time*? It's by Allie Louyah.

****

"Mum, Mum! I keep running in circles." "Shut up or I'll nail your other foot to the floor."

****

There once was a juggler named Drops
Who couldn't hang on to his props.
He tossed 'em and heaved 'em,
Then dropped and retrieved 'em,
Till the audience told him to stop.

What is a Chinese seven-course dinner? Six bowls of rice and a cooked rat.

****

What is a Japanese seven-course dinner? A bowl of rice and six raw fish.

****

What is a Russian seven-course dinner? A litre of vodka and six turnips.

****

What is a Mexican seven-course dinner? A bottle of Tequila and six cockroaches.

****

What is an Eskimo seven-course dinner? Six lumps of snow and a baby seal.

****

How many proofreaders does it take to change a lightbulb? Proofreaders aren't supposed to change lightbulbs. They should just query them.

****

How many armies does it take to change a lightbulb? At least six: the Germans to start it; the French to give up really easily after only trying for a little while; the Italians to make a start, get nowhere, and then run away; the English to stand firm back home but not get anywhere near the bulb; the Americans to turn up late, finish it off and take all the credit; and the Swiss to pretend nothing out of the ordinary is happening.

****

What is an Argentine seven-course dinner? Six cuts of beef and a sprig of parsley.

****

How many sheep does it take to change a lightbulb? Twenty-one: one to change it and twenty to follow him round while he looks for a new one.

****

What is an English seven-course dinner? Three pints of lager, two packs of crisps, a bag of chips and a doner kebab.

****

What is an Irish seven-course dinner? A four-pack of Guinness and a potato.

****

Have you heard about the new book, *A Map of the Brain*? It's by Sarah Bellum.

****

Have you heard about the new book, *Nudist Beaches of the South Coast*? It's by Seymour Butts.

****

Have you heard about the new book, *Real Ales of the United Kingdom*? It's by Bart Enda.

****

Have you heard about the new book, *The Case Of The Missing Will*? It's by Benny Fishery.

****

How many MPs does it take to change a lightbulb? Twenty-one: one to change it and twenty to take a six-week fact-finding trip to the Bahamas to learn more about how it's done.

****

Have you heard about the new book, *The Encyclopaedia of Mixers*? It's by Ginger Aile.

****

Have you heard about the new book, *Beating The Mortgage Trap*? It's by Bill Jerome Holmes.

****

"Mum, Mum! The milkman's here. Have you got the money or should I go out and play?"

****

How many lawyers does it take to change a light bulb? Three: one to sue the power company for insufficiently supplying power, or negligent failure to prevent the surge that made the bulb burn out in the first place; one to sue the electrician who wired the house; and one to sue the bulb manufacturers.

****

"Mum, Mum! What's a nymphomaniac?" "Shut up and help me get Gran off the doorknob!"

****

Have you heard about the new book, *The Pizza Man*? It's by Pepe Rooney.

Have you heard about the new book, *Italian Cookery Made Simple*? It's by Les Anya.

****

How many trainspotters does it take to change a lightbulb? Three: one to change it; one to write down its serial number; and one to bring the anoraks and the flask of soup.

****

Have you heard about the new book, *Savaged by Lions – A Survivial Story*? It's by Claudia Armoff.

****

"Mum, Mum! Why don't I have a big thing like Dad's between my legs?" "You will when you're older, Lucy!"

****

How many Belgians does it take to change a lightbulb? Two: one to change it and one to serve it with chips and mayonnaise.

****

How many divorcees does it take to change a lightbulb? None: the sockets all went with the house.

****

How many gardeners does it take to change a lightbulb? Three: one to change it and two to have a debate about whether they should be putting in light bulbs or crocus bulbs.

****

How many thieves does it take to change a lightbulb? None, but you lose a lot of light bulbs.

****

How many Italians does it take to change a lightbulb? Two: one to change it and one to sprinkle it with Parmesan.

****

How many new-agers does it take to change a lightbulb? Two: one to change it and one to check the Feng Shui of the new one.

****

How many politicians does it take to change a lightbulb? Four: one to change it and the other three to deny it was ever changed.

****

How many sexists does it take to change a lightbulb? None: let the bitch cook in the dark.

****

How many Thatcherites does it take to change a lightbulb? None: it's up to the private sector to change it.

****

There was a young man from Bellaire
Who was screwing his girl on the stair.
But the bannister broke,
So he doubled his stroke,
And he finished her off in mid-air.

****

How many Trotskyites does it take to change a lightbulb? It's no use trying to CHANGE it brothers, it's got to be SMASHED.

How many christians does it take to change a light bulb? Three: but they're really only one, so that's okay.

****

How many consultants does it take to change a light bulb? Only one: but it takes eight months at £150 a day.

****

How many dogs does it take to change a light bulb? Two: one to change it, and one to sniff the first one's arse.

****

How many firemen does it take to change a light bulb? Four: one to change the bulb and three to cut a hole in the roof.

****

How many jugglers does it take to change a light bulb? Only one: but it takes at least three light bulbs.

****

Why did the mormon groom cross the road? To get to the other bride.

"Mum, Mum! Are you sure this is how to learn to swim?" "Shut up and get back in the sack."

****

"Mum, Mum! What's an Oedipus complex?" "Shut up and kiss me."

****

"Mum, Mum! Why can't I play with the other kids?" "Shut up and deal."

****

Have you heard about the new book, *Without Warning*? It's by Oliver Sodden.

****

Have you heard about the new book, *Great Presents*? It's by Sue Pryse.

****

Have you heard about the new book, *Tending Lawns*? It's by Leif Raker.

Have you heard about the new book, *Beating Stress*? It's by Neddy Tate.

****

Have you heard about the new book, *Medieval Music*? It's by Manda Lynn.

****

Have you heard about the new book, *Medical Process*? It's by Steffi Scope.

****

Have you heard about the new book, *Spanish Bloodsports*? It's by Matt Adore.

****

Have you heard about the new book, *Prediction Explained*? It's by Claire Voiant.

****

How did the priest make the road a cross? He painted another line.

Have you heard about the new book, *Fitted Carpets*? It's by Walter Wall.

****

Have you heard about the new book, *Daylight Robbery*? It's by Hans Zupp.

****

Have you heard about the new book, *Dangerous Maniacs*? It's by Si Cosis.

****

Have you heard about the new book, *Being Prepared*? It's by Everett D Reddy.

****

Have you heard about the new book, *Breakfast Cookery*? It's by Hammond Degs.

****

Have you heard about the new book, *After Life*? It's by Doug Graves.

Have you heard about the new book, *Helping Others*? It's by Linda Hand.

****

Have you heard about the new book, *Fitness Explained*? It's by Jim Nasium.

****

How do you spoil a cat? Leave it out in the sun.

****

Have you heard about the new book, *Mortgages Explained*? It's by Owen Moony.

****

Have you heard about the new book, *Security Measures*? It's by Barb Dwyer.

****

Have you heard about the new book, *Police Brutality*? It's by Lauren Order.

Have you heard about the new book, *Buying Music*? It's by Chopin Liszt.

****

Have you heard about the new book, *Perfect Parties*? It's by Greg Arius.

****

Have you heard about the new book, *Religious Governments*? It's by Dick Tater.

****

Why did the chicken cross the road? To see his friend Gregory Peck.

****

"Mum, Mum! I don't want to empty the compost heap." "Shut up and keep eating."

****

Have you heard about the new book, *The Worker's Guide to Shirking*? It's by Hans Doolittle.

Have you heard about the new book, *New Age Gemstones*? It's by Chris Tall.

****

"Mum, Mum! Grandpa's going out!" "Well throw some more petrol on him then."

****

What is worse than a dead cat in a dustbin? Ten dead cats in a dustbin.

****

Have you heard about the new book, *Free Yourself From Pain*? It's by Ann L Gesick.

****

"Mum, Mum! What happened to all that dog food Fido wouldn't eat?" "Shut up and eat your meat loaf."

****

Have you heard about the new book, *The Long Fall*? It's by Eileen Dover and Phil Down.

Have you heard about the new book, *Nuclear Fission Explained*? It's by Adam Bohm.

****

Have you heard about the new book, *Heroin: The Evil Pleasure*? It's by Anita Fyx.

****

"Mum, Mum! When are we going to have Aunt Edna for dinner?" "Shut up, we haven't finished your Grandmother yet."

****

"Mum, Mum! Dad just poisoned my kitten!" "Never mind dear. Perhaps he had to do it." "No he didn't, he promised me I could!"

****

What is easier to unload, a truck full of dead cats or a truck full of bowling balls? Dead cats, because you can use a pitchfork.

****

What's more fun than nailing a cat to a fence? Ripping it back off.

A popular girl is Miss Cholmondeley,
She's youthful, attractive and comely,
And never objects
To suggestions of sex,
But simply cooperates dumbly.

****

Why did the rabbit cross the road? Because the chicken retired and moved to Florida.

****

What is a German seven-course dinner? Six different beers and kilo of raw sausage.

****

Why did the Koala fall out of the tree? Because it was dead.

****

"Mum, Mum! Sally won't come skipping with me." "Don't be cruel dear, you know it makes her stumps bleed."

****

What goes plink, plink, fizz? Kittens in an acid bath.

****

Why did the chicken cross the road? To get away from Colonel Sanders.

****

The sea captain's tender young bride
Fell into the sea at low tide.
You could tell by her squeals
That one of the eels
Had found her the best place to hide.

****

"Mum, Mum! What's a vampire?" "Shut up and eat your soup before it clots."

****

"Mum, Mum! What's an orgasm?" "I don't know dear, ask your father."

****

There was an old man from Australia
Who painted his arse like a dahlia.
The colours were fine,
Likewise the design,
But the smell, alas, was a failure.

****

"Mum, Mum! Dad's running down the street!" "Shut up and step on the accelerator!"

****

How many aerospace engineers does it take to change a light bulb? None: it doesn't take a rocket scientist, you know.

****

How many art directors does it take to change a lightbulb? Does it have to be a lightbulb?

****

"Mum, Mum! Why do I have to hop everywhere?" "Shut up or I'll chop off the other leg!"

How many social workers does it take to change a lightbulb? Four: one to remove the bulb from the socket and take it away without checking whether or not there was actually anything wrong with it: one to accuse its owners of mistreating it: one to find somewhere else to screw it in for the next six months: and one to eventually bring it back and say it was all done with the lightbulb's best interests at heart.

****

What is the difference between a pregnant woman and a light bulb? You can unscrew a light bulb.

****

What do you do with four dead cats and a sheet of glass? Make a coffee table.

****

"Mum, Mum! Can I wear a bra now I'm 16?" "Shut up, Albert."

****

Have you heard the Hypnotist's answering machine? It says: "You're growing tired. Your eyelids are getting heavy. You feel very sleepy now. You are gradually losing your willpower and your ability to resist suggestions. When you hear the tone you will feel helplessly compelled to leave your name, number, and a message."

****

What is an anorexic seven-course dinner? Six peas and a sip of water.

****

"Mum, Mum! I don't want to see Niagara falls!" "Shut up and get back in the barrel!"

****

"Mum, Mum! I don't want to go to Australia." "Shut up and keep swimming."

****

Have you heard the lunatic's answering machine? It says: "Hi, I'm not sane right now, but if you leave your name, number and shoe size at the sound of the tone, I'll get back to you when and if I return to my senses."

****

Anything that doesn't eat you today is saving you for tomorrow.

****

A short cut is the longest distance between two points.

****

If you do not care where you are, then you aren't lost.

****

One of those days? I have one of those lives.

****

Beware of altruism. It is based on self-deception, the root of all evil.

****

After things have gone from bad to worse, the cycle will repeat itself.

****

When it's you against the world, bet on the world.

All I ask is the chance to prove that money cannot make me happy.

****

Anyone can admit they were wrong; the true test is admitting it to someone else.

****

You Know You're Getting Old When... A fortune teller offers to read your face.

****

Old age and treachery shall overcome youth and talent.

****

Eat the rich. The poor are tough and stringy.

****

He who dies with the most toys is still dead.

****

What is orange and sleeps five? A council road-repair van.

****

You can fool some of the people and really piss them off.

****

The race is not always to the swift nor the battle to the strong, but that's the way to bet.

****

You Know You're Getting Old When... You feel like the morning after but there was no night before.

****

Information travels more surely to those with a lesser need to know.

****

The sun goes down just when you need it the most.

****

Pessimists have already begun to worry about what is going to replace automation.

****

Almost everything in life is easier to get into than to get out of.

****

You Know You're Getting Old When... The gleam in your eyes is from the sun hitting your bifocals.

****

If at first you do succeed, try to hide your astonishment.

****

If everything seems to be going well, you have obviously overlooked something.

****

If there is a possibility of several things going wrong, the one that will cause the most damage will be the one to go wrong.

Never do anything you wouldn't be caught dead doing.

****

You Know You're Getting Old When... Your birthday cake collapses from the weight of the candles.

****

It's always darkest just before it goes pitch black.

****

If ignorance is bliss, most of us must be orgasmic.

****

Left to themselves, things tend to go from bad to worse.

****

Money is better than poverty, if only for financial reasons.

****

The idea is to die young as late as possible.

You Know You're Getting Old When... You regret all those mistakes resisting temptation.

****

Don't be so open minded that your brain falls out.

****

Some come to the fountain of knowledge to drink, some prefer to just gargle.

****

Blessed are those who go around in circles, for they shall be known as wheels.

****

It is impossible to make anything foolproof, because fools are so ingenious.

****

If anything just cannot go wrong, it will anyway.

For every action, there is a corresponding over-reaction.

****

Anybody can win, unless there happens to be a second entry.

****

Everything tastes more or less like chicken.

****

Beware the fury of a patient man.

****

Common sense is not so common.

****

Assumption is the mother of all foul-ups.

****

Two heads are more numerous than one.

Don't lend people money...it gives them amnesia.

****

A penny saved is virtually worthless.

****

Everything in moderation, including moderation.

****

No good deed goes unpunished.

****

Friends come and go, but enemies accumulate.

****

A closed mouth gathers no foot.

****

When all else fails, read the instructions.

Change is inevitable, except from a vending machine.

****

Even paranoids have enemies.

****

Sometimes too much drink is not enough.

****

Winning isn't everything, but losing isn't anything.

****

The bigger they are, the harder they hit.

****

I think...therefore I am confused.

****

Familiarity breeds children.

Around the pub

7

Jokes about Food, Music, Sport and Old People in the Corner

IN THE RESTAURANT

A family of three tomatoes are walking downtown one day when the little baby tomato starts lagging behind. The big father tomato walks back to the baby tomato, stomps on her, squashing her into a red paste, and says, “Ketchup!”

****

One day, Bill and Tom went to a restaurant for dinner. As soon as the waiter brought out two steaks, Bill quickly picked out the bigger steak for himself. Tom wasn’t happy about that, asking: “When are you going to learn to be polite?” Bill replied “If you had the chance to pick first, which one would you pick?” Tom said: “The smaller piece, of course.” Bill sneered: “What are you mumbling about then? Then the smaller piece is what you want, right?”

****

“Here waiter, my plate’s wet!” “That’s not wet, sir – that’s the soup!”

****

A customer was bothering the waiter in a restaurant. First, he asked that the air conditioning be turned up because he was too hot, then he asked it be turned down because he was too cold, and so on for about half an hour. Surprisingly, the waiter was very patient. He walked back and forth and never once got angry. So finally, a second customer asked him why he didn't throw out the pest. "Oh I don't care," said the waiter with a smile, "we don't even have an air conditioner."

****

"Here waiter, have you got asparagus?" "We don't serve sparrows and my name is not Gus!"

****

"Here waiter, this coffee is horrible." "Don't complain, sir. You may be old and weak yourself some day."

****

One day, Johnny asked: "Daddy, are caterpillars good to eat?" His father was irritated. "I've told you not to talk about things like that during meals." "Why did you want to know?" asked his mother. Johnny said: "It's because I saw one on daddy's lettuce, but now it's gone."

****

"Here waiter, this bun tastes of soap." "Yes sir – it's a Bath bun."

"Here waiter, what do you call this?" "That's bean soup, sir." "I don't care what it's been, what is it now?"

****

"Here waiter, what do you call this?" "Cottage pie, sir." "Well, I've just bitten on a piece of the door."

****

"Here waiter, there's no chicken in this chicken pie." "So what? You don't get dog in a dog biscuit, do you?"

****

"Here waiter, what's the meaning of this fly in my tea-cup?" "I wouldn't know, sir. I'm a waiter, not a fortune-teller."

****

"Here waiter, if this is plaice then I'm an idiot." "You're right, sir – it is plaice."

****

What is the most common speech impediment? Chewing gum.

"Here waiter, this egg tastes rather strong." "Never mind, sir, the tea's nice and weak."

****

"Here waiter, this soup tastes funny." "So why aren't you laughing then, sir?"

****

"Here waiter, how long will my sausages be?" "Oh, about three or four inches if you're lucky."

****

A man in a restaurant orders chicken noodle soup. He starts to eat the soup and chokes on a hair in it. After gagging for a minute, he calls the waitress. "I'm not paying for this soup. There was a hair in it." The waitress and customer get into a bit of an argument over the problem. The man ends up storming out of the restaurant without paying. The waitress sees him go across the street to a house of ill repute. The waitress's shift finishes and she hurries over to the house, finds out where the man is and interrupts his evening of pleasure. As she walks in, she sees the man with his face in the hooker's business area. "You wouldn't pay for the chicken noodle soup because you found hair in it. Now look where your face is." The man pulls his face out of the muff, turns to the waitress and says, “And if I find a noodle in there, I will not pay for that either.”

****

“Here waiter, does the pianist play requests?” “Yes, sir.” “Then ask him to play tiddlywinks till I’ve finished my meal.”

****

“Here waiter, I’ll have the pie, please.” “Anything with it, sir?” “If it’s anything like last time I’d better have a hammer and chisel.”

****

Clearly it is not the lovelorn sufferer who seeks solace in chocolate, but rather the chocolate-deprived individual, who, desperate, seeks in mere love a pale approximation of bittersweet euphoria.

****

“Here waiter, this lobster’s only got one claw.” “I expect he’s been in a fight, sir.” “Well, bring me the winner!”

****

"Here waiter, that dog's just run off with my roast lamb!" "Yes, it's very popular, sir."

****

"Here waiter, bring me a glass of milk and a Dover sole." "Fillet?" "Yes, to the brim."

****

"Here waiter, bring me a fried egg with finger-marks in it, some luke-warm greasy chips and a portion of watery cabbage." "We don't do food like that, sir!" "You did yesterday..."

****

"Here waiter, I'll pay my bill now." "I'm afraid this £10 note is bad, sir." "So what? So was the meal."

****

"Here waiter, I'll have a chop; no – make that a steak." "I'm a waiter, sir, not a magician!"

****

"Here waiter, there's a bird in my soup." "That's all right, sir. It's bird's nest soup."

****

"Here waiter, there's a hair in my honey." "It must have dropped off the comb, sir!"

****

"Here waiter, there's a fly in my soup." "That's all right, sir, he won't drink much."

****

"Here waiter, send the chef here. I want to complain about this disgusting meal." "I'm afraid you'll have to wait, sir. He's just popped out for his dinner."

****

"Here waiter, there's a beetle in my soup. Get me the manager." "That won't do any good, sir – he's frightened of them as well!"

****

"Here waiter, there's a fly in my soup." "Couldn't be, sir. The cook used them all in the raisin bread."

****

"Here waiter, there's a worm on my plate." "That's your sausage, sir."

****

"Here waiter, this coffee tastes like mud!" "I'm not surprised, sir, it was ground only a few minutes ago."

****

"Here waiter, bring me tea without milk." "We haven't any milk, sir. How about tea without cream?"

****

"Here waiter, have you got frogs' legs?" "Certainly, sir." "Then hop into the kitchen and get me a steak!"

****

"Here waiter, there's a fly swimming in my soup." "What do you expect me to do, call a lifeguard?"

"Here waiter, there's a dead fly in my soup!" "Yes, sir, it's the hot water that kills them."

****

"Here waiter, there's a dead fly in my soup." "What do you expect for £4 – a live one?"

****

"Here waiter, this bread's got sand in it." "That's to stop the butter slipping off, sir."

****

A friend got vinegar in his ear, now he suffers from pickled hearing.

****

"Here waiter, there is a fly in my soup." "Sorry sir, I must have missed it when I removed the other three."

****

"Here waiter, there is a fly in my salad." "I'm sorry sir, I didn't know that you were vegetarian."

A guy goes to visit his aunt in the nursing home. It turns out she's napping so he just sits down in a chair in her room, flips through a few magazines, and munches on some peanuts sitting in a bowl on the table. Eventually, the aunt wakes up, and her nephew realizes he's absentmindedly finished the entire bowl. "I'm so sorry, auntie, I've eaten all of your peanuts!" "That's okay, dearie," the aunt replied. "After I've sucked the chocolate off, I don't care for them anyway."

****

"Here waiter. Bring me a crocodile sandwich, and make it snappy."

****

"Here waiter, there is a mosquito in my soup." "Yes sir, I'm afraid we've run out of flies."

****

"Here waiter, waiter, is this a hair in my soup?" "Why, of course sir. That's rabbit stew!"

****

"Here waiter, is this all you've got to eat?" "No, sir, I'll be having a nice shepherd's pie when I get home."

"Here waiter, waiter, is this a fly in my soup?" "Quite possibly, sir. The chef used to be a tailor."

****

"Here waiter, I'll have soup and then fish." "I'd have the fish first if I were you, sir, it's just on the turn."

****

"Here waiter, my bill please." "How did you find your luncheon, sir?" "With a magnifying glass."

****

I know about stressed... It's desserts spelled backwards.

****

"Here waiter, is this a lamb chop or a pork chop?" "Can't you tell by the taste?" "No, I can't." "Well what does it matter, then?"

****

A man walks into a Chinese restaurant but is told that there will be at least a 20 minute wait and he is asked if he would like to wait in the bar. He goes into the bar and the bartender says, "What'll it be?" The man replies, "Give me a Stoli with a twist." The bartender squints at him for a few seconds, then smiles and says: "Once upon time there were four little pigs..."

****

"Here waiter, how long have you been here?" "Six months, sir." "Ah, then it can't be you who took my order."

****

"Here waiter, I think I'd like a little game." "Draughts or tiddlywinks, sir?"

****

"Here waiter, do you call this a three-course meal?" "That's right, sir. Two chips and a pea."

****

"Tea or coffee, gentlemen?" asked the waiter. "I'll have tea," said one bloke. "Me, too," said his mate, "and make sure the glass is clean." The waiter returned shortly afterwards, saying "Two teas. Which of you asked for the clean glass?"

THE JUKE BOX

Two violinists make a pact that whoever dies first will contact the other and tell him what life in heaven is like. Poor Max has a heart attack and dies. He manages to make contact with Abe the next day. Abe says: "I can't believe this worked. What is it like in Heaven?" Max replies: "Well, it's great, but I've got good news, and I've got bad news. The good news is that there's a fantastic orchestra up here, and in fact, we're playing "Sheherazade", your favourite piece, tomorrow night." Abe says: "So what's the bad news?" Max replies: "Well, you're booked to play the solo."

****

Vibrato: the singer's equivalent of an epileptic seizure.

****

What is the definition of a Soviet string quartet? A Soviet symphony orchestra after a tour of the USA.

****

What is the range of a tuba? Twenty yards, if you've got a good arm.

A harp is a nude piano.

****

English horn: a woodwind that got its name because it's neither English nor a horn. Not to be confused with the French horn, which is German.

****

Agnus Dei was a woman composer famous for her church music.

****

Trombone: a slide whistle with delusions of grandeur.

****

Chord: usually spelled with an "s" on the end, means a particular type of trousers, eg "he wears chords."

****

Rubber bands are musicians who believe in safe sex.

****

Metronome: a dwarf who lives in the city.

****

Tempo: this is where a headache begins.

****

Why don't they know where Mozart is buried? Because he's Haydn.

****

Why do bagpipers walk when they play? To get away from the noise.

****

What do you get when you drop a piano down a mine shaft? A flat minor.

****

What do you get when you cross a Mafia lieutenant and a performance artist? Someone who makes you an offer that you can't understand.

****

What do you get when an army officer puts his nose to the grindstone? A sharp major.

****

What do you get when you play a new-age song backwards? Another new-age song.

****

A soprano died and went to heaven. St Peter stopped her at the gate and asked: "well, how many false notes did you sing in your life?" The soprano answers: "three." "Three times, fellows," says St Peter, and along comes an angel and sticks the soprano three times with a needle. "Ow! What was that for?" asks the soprano. St Peter explains, "here in heaven, we stick you once for each false note you've sung down on Earth." "Oh," says the soprano, and is just about to step through the gates when she suddenly hears a horrible screaming from behind a door. "Oh my goodness, what is THAT?" asks the soprano, horrified. "That," says St Peter, "is a tenor we got some time back. He's just about to start his third week in the sewing machine."

****

Gregorian chant: a way of singing in unison, invented by monks to hide snoring.

What do you get if Bach falls off a horse, but has the courage to get on again and continue riding? Bach in the saddle again.

****

Real musicians don't die, they just decompose.

****

Music sung by two people at the same time is called a duel.

****

Did you hear about the female opera singer who had quite a range at the lower end of the scale. She was known as the deep C diva.

****

Have you heard about the new American radio station called WPMS? Each month, they play two weeks of love songs, one week of blues, one week of ragtime, and two days of death metal.

****

It is easy to teach anyone to play the maracas. Just grip the neck and shake him in rhythm.

One evening, after a symphony rehearsal, some of the players went out to Sam's Discotheque to unwind. After several relaxing drinks, they all went their separate ways home. The next night, the harpist showed up at the concert hall and realized that he didn't have his instrument. "Oh no," he cried, "I left my harp in Sam's damn disco..."

****

Beat: what music students do to each other with their musical instruments. The down beat is performed on the top of the head, while the up beat is struck under the chin.

****

Rhythmic drone: the sound of many monks suffering with crotchet.

****

Dad, why do the singers rock left and right while performing on stage? Because, son, it is more difficult to hit a moving target.

****

Refrain means don't do it. A refrain in music is the part you had better not try to sing.

How many tenors does it take to change a light bulb? Six. One to do it, and five to say, "it's too high for HIM."

****

How many altos does it take to change a light bulb? None. They can't get up that high.

****

A trumpet is an instrument when it is not an elephant sound.

****

Band members do it in front of 100,000 people.

****

Woodwind players do it in the reeds.

****

An eccentric lady was in need of a piano player for her forthcoming party. She placed ads and spread the word but could not find a suitable one. A bum knocked on her door and when she saw the state of his condition, she answered, "go away." He said: "please, won't you just give me a chance, I'm a piano player." She was desperate so she let him in. After his performance, she couldn't believe her ears. "Wow! That sounded great, best I've heard in years. What was the name of that song?" The bum answered, "oh, it's called 'I Love Me Wife So Much I Took A Big Dump'." "Oh," said the lady, "how unusual, would you play another?" He proceeded to play another tune and again she was astounded by the performance. "That was fantastic," she said. "What was the name of that tune?" "That one is called 'I Took My Wife From Behind And Made A Mess All Over That Carpet'." Again she commented: "how unusual." She went to say: "you've got the job, but if anyone asks the names of your songs, please don't tell them. And do something about your clothes; you look terrible. Go and buy a tux for the party." The bum was happy about his new job and happy to buy a tuxedo, but, as he had never bought one before, he wound up getting one that was three sizes too small. At the big party, the crowd was amazed at his performance. He bowed at the crowd back and forth and ripped out the whole rear end of his trousers. One lady stepped forward clapping and said, "sir, you are a great piano player but do you know you have a hairy ass and your balls are hanging out?" With a smile, the bum replied, "lady, know it? I wrote it."

****

A tourist is sightseeing in a European city. She comes upon the tomb of Beethoven, and begins reading the commemorative plaque, only to be distracted by a low scratching noise, as if something were rubbing against a piece of paper. She collars a passing native and asks what the scratching sound is. The local person replies: "Oh, that is Beethoven. He's decomposing."

****

How can you tell if a violin is out of tune? The bow is moving.

****

What do you get if you run over an army officer with a steam roller? A flat major.

****

What do you say to an army officer while your running him over with a steam roller? Be flat, major.

****

What do you say after you've run over an army officer with a steam roller? See, flat major.

****

A musical reviewer admitted he always praised the first show of a new theatrical season. "Who am I to stone the first cast?"

****

A Celtic harpist spends half her time tuning her harp, and the other half playing it out of tune.

****

Opera is when a guy gets stabbed in the back and, instead of bleeding, he sings.

****

What is another name for a bassoon? A farting bedpost.

****

"Haven't I seen your face before?" a judge demanded, looking down at the defendant. "You have, your Honour," the man answered hopefully, "I gave your son violin lessons last winter." "Ah, yes," recalled the judge. "Twenty years!"

****

How many sound men does it take to change a light bulb? One, two, three, testing, one, two, one, two.

****

Quaver: beginning violin class.

****

Crotchet: it's like knitting, but faster.

****

A cowboy and a biker are on Death Row, and are to be executed on the same day. The day comes, and they are brought to the gas chamber. The warden asks the cowboy if he has a last request, to which the cowboy replies: "ah shore do, wardn. Ah'd be mighty grateful if'n yoo'd play 'Achy Breaky Heart' fur me bahfore ah hafta go." "Sure enough, cowboy, we can do that," says the warden. He turns to the biker, "and you, biker, what's your last request?" "That you kill me first."

****

What is the difference between a violin and a viola? The viola holds more beer.

What is the difference between a saxophone and a chainsaw? It's all in the grip.

****

What is the difference between a bull and an orchestra? The bull has the horns in front and the arsehole in the back.

****

While at a concert being performed by a very bad orchestra, George Bernard Shaw was asked what he'd like them to play next. "Dominoes," he replied.

****

Person 1: "It must be terrible for an opera singer to realize that he can never sing again". Person 2: "Yes, but it's much more terrible if he doesn't realize it."

****

Seems that the censors banned the transmission of a TV show that claimed to introduce young people to the worlds of jazz and classical music. Their reasoning? Too much sax and violins.

An accordion is a bagpipe with pleats.

****

Disco is to music what Etch-A-Sketch is to art.

****

This guy says to his wife, "oh, baby. I can play you just like a violin." His wife says, "But I'd rather have you play me like a harmonica."

****

How do you get a guitar player to play softer? Give him a sheet of music. How do you make him stop playing altogether? Put notes on it.

****

How do you get five oboists in tune? Shoot four of them.

****

Semiconductors are part-time musicians.

****

A musician dies of a heroin overdose, and finds himself in purgatory. There, he meets an angel who is reading a large book with his name on the cover. The angel looks up at the newly arrived spirit and says: "hi, we've been expecting you." "Where am I?" asks the musician. "In purgatory," the angel answers. "I've been reading the book of your life, and your good deeds are evenly balanced by your bad deeds." "So, what's next?" "We've decided to let you pick where you are going, heaven or hell. And, to help you make up your mind, we're going to give you a glimpse of each." So saying, the angel motions the musician over to a curtain labelled "heaven". The angel parts the curtain, and before them is a bucolic scene of eternal spring with angelic choirs singing praises to God. The musician surveys the scene, and says, "well, I could hang with that. But...what's hell look like?" In response, the angel motions the musician over to a curtain labelled "hell". Parting the curtain reveals a smoke filled room with well-dressed people happily talking and dancing, while a quartet is playing a rather good version of "*Have You Met Miss Jones?*" "Well, to tell you the truth," says the musician, "I've got nothing against heaven, but hell looks like a place that I could really dig." "No problem," answers the angel. With that, he pulls an unseen lever and the musician falls through a trap door. The musician lands with a large splash in a cauldron of boiling blood. There are screams of eternal agony in the distance. A horribly ugly demon begins poking the musician in the side with a large trident. "What's this?" cries the musician. "I've been tricked!" The demon answers, "Yeah, I know. But that thing up there sure is a top demo tape, eh?"

SPORT ON THE BOX

"I didn't see you in church last Sunday, Nigel. I hear you were out playing football instead." "That's not true, vicar. And I've got the fish to prove it."

****

If at first you don't succeed, skydiving is not your sport.

****

Hunters do it with a bang.

****

Remember the days when sex was safe and skydiving was dangerous?

****

A priest was walking along the cliffs at Dover when he came upon two locals pulling another man ashore on the end of a rope. "That's what I like to see," said the priest, "a man helping his fellow man." As he was walking away, one local remarked to the other: "well, he sure doesn't know the first thing about shark fishing."

"He's great on the court," a sportswriter said of a college basketball player in an interview with his coach, "but how's his scholastic work?" "Why, he makes straight '"A"s," replied the coach. "Wonderful!" said the sportswriter. "Yes," agreed the coach, "but his '"B"s are a little crooked."

****

In Africa, some of the native tribes have a custom of beating the ground with clubs and uttering spine-chilling cries. Anthropologists call this a form of primitive self-expression. In Britain we call it golf.

****

A minister is out playing a round of golf one day with three of his friends, who are also ministers, when, on one of the par fives he reaches the edge of the green in three, leaving himself with about a 35-40 foot birdie putt. He lines the putt up so that he feels pretty comfortable with it and strikes what looks to be a perfect putt, headed straight for the hole. Just as the ball gets to the hole, it stops, hanging right on the rim of the hole. Being a preacher and a man of God, he looks up to the sky and says to God, "how about a little help?" Just as he says this, a moth flies onto the green, briefly buzzes around their heads and then decides to rest right on his ball, but the ball still doesn't move. So he says: "you didn't send a big enough moth." Just as he says this, the moth starts crawling around the ball, and eventually crawls to the hole side of the ball, causing the ball to drop straight into the hole. The minister simply looks up to the sky and says: “amen!”

****

Man with unchecked parachute will leap to conclusion.

****

You know you’ve made the right decision to take up jogging if, on your first try at it, you have more jiggle than jog.

****

There’s a fine line between fishing and standing on the shore looking like an idiot.

****

When another foursome is on the green, “fore!” is not an excuse, “so what?” is not an apology, and “up yours!” is not an explanation.

****

Old hunters never die, they just stay loaded.

Golf is a game that needlessly prolongs the lives of some of our most useless citizens.

****

Tennis players have fuzzy balls.

****

Fishermen do it for reel.

****

Taffy gets his first golf lesson. His instructor tells him: "you see that little flagpole over there. Just hit the ball and try to get it as close to it as you can." So Taffy gives it a good whack and upon approaching the hole they see that he has ended up 5cm from the hole. "Very good," the instructor says amazed. "Now, you have to hit it into the hole." "What!" exclaims Taffy. "Why didn't you say so in the first place?"

****

To catch the fish, it's not how you throw the bait, but how you wiggle your worm.

****

Golfers have it down to a tee.

****

After spending all day watching football, Harry fell asleep in front of the rugby and spent the whole night in the chair. In the morning, his wife woke him up. "Get up dear," she said, "it's twenty to seven." He awoke with a start and said, "to who?"

****

A man books into a new and fancy resort which advertises an all-inclusive do-all-you-can kind of holiday. Looking through the hotel's book, he finds there are tennis courts on the premises so he calls the desk to find out how to go about playing a set or two. "Just meet the pro at the tennis shop, he will lend you all that you need and will find you someone to play with." "How much is that going to cost me?" the man asks. "Nothing, this is on the room," answers a very polite clerk. So the man plays tennis all afternoon. The next day he decides to try horseback riding and again finds it doesn't cost him a penny more than the price of the room. After a week at the hotel he has done just about everything that's available except golf. On his last day, he decides to play a round so he goes to the clubhouse, gets what he needs and starts his game. At the end of his round the pro asks him how the game went. "Not so good," the man answers, "in fact I lost five balls." "Well," says the pro, "that will be £5000 sir." "What do you mean £5000, for five damn golf balls? You have to be kidding. I played an afternoon of tennis, went horse riding, scuba diving, deep-sea fishing and more, and was never charged a cent. Now that I have lost five balls you charge me £5000." "Well," says the pro, "you know, this hotel really gets you by the balls."

****

Why do mountain climbers rope themselves together? To prevent the sensible ones from going home.

****

What's the difference between a hockey game and all-in wrestling? In a hockey game, the fights are real.

****

All morning, the American businessman talks about golf in his office. The rest of the day, he discusses work on the golf course.

****

Did you hear about the moron who went elephant hunting? He got a hernia carrying the decoys.

THE OLD CODGER AT THE BAR

A bloke gives his 85-year-old father a surprise visit from a whore as a birthday present. He answers the door, and she bubbles at him: "hi, I'm here to give you super sex." He looks at her for a moment, and replies: "um, thanks, I'll have the soup."

****

If you reach 90, you can help advance medical science. There isn't much we know about sex at that age. Rats don't live that long...

****

Two elderly men are sitting at the bar, watching the young girls go by. One says to the other: "you know, I'm still sexually interested in women. In fact, I always get excited when I see the young girls walking by. The real problem is that at this age, I don't see so well any more."

****

A couple in their late sixties decide to marry (their respective spouses having died), and move to Bournemouth. In preparation for this they talk through the sharing of household expenses and various other matters. Jane asks Harold what they should do about their present houses. "Well, we ought to each sell our home and then we can each fund half the purchase price of our new home." Jane agrees. Harold then asks Jane what she'd like to do about the grocery bills. She suggests: "neither one of us eats very much, so maybe we ought to split that bill on a monthly basis." Harold agrees. Then what about the utility bill? Again, they decide to share. Then Jane asks Harold what he wants to do about sex, to which he replies: "Oh, infrequently." Jane looks at him and asks: "is that one word or two?"

****

What dominates the thoughts of men at different stages in their lives

Age	Primary Concerns
0-3	Shitting and drooling
4-10	Shitting and drooling
11-15	Sex and beer
16-20	Sex and beer
20-40	Sex and beer
40-60	Sex and beer
60-80	Sex and beer
80-?	Shitting and drooling

****

What dominates the thoughts of women at different stages in their lives

Age	Primary Concerns
0-3	Shitting and drooling
4-10	Dolls and shopping
11-15	Periods and shopping
16-20	Sex and shopping
20-40	Shopping and shopping
40-60	Getting old and wrinkly, and shopping
60-80	The price of coal and shopping
80-?	Whinging and shopping

****

An elderly man and his wife decided to separate. Before being allowed to do so legally, the Family Court insisted that they undergo some counselling from the marriage guidance mob, to see if their union could be saved. The counsellor did her best, but to no avail. The old folk were absolutely determined to go through with separation leading to divorce. Finally, in some desperation, the counsellor said: "But you're 95 and your wife is 93. You've been married for 72 years. Why do you want to separate now?" The wife replied, "we haven't been able to stand each other for the last 46 years, but we thought we should wait until all the children died before we split up."

****

An elderly man tells the doctor he is planning to marry a women aged 30 and asks if he has any suggestions. "Yes," says the doctor, "I would advise you to take in a lodger." A year later, at his eightieth birthday check-up, the doctor asks how everything is going. The man says: "fine; my wife is pregnant." The doctor remarks, "so you took my advice and took in a lodger?" "Yes I did," comes the reply, "and she's pregnant as well."

****

An old man marries a girl barely out of her teens. Needless to say she is pretty horny, so when they get into bed on the wedding night she asks him: "so are we going to have rampant sex tonight?" The man responds by raising his hand and outstretching his fingers. "What? Five times?" asks the eager girl. "No," he replies, "pick a finger."

****

You're not from round 'ere, are you?

8

Jokes about Wales, Cornwall and Essex girls

I heard they closed the zoo in Cardiff... The duck died.

****

Why are Essex girls' coffins Y-shaped? Because as soon as they are on their backs, their legs open.

****

How do you know when you're flying over Wales? You see toilet paper hanging on the clothes lines.

****

Following the assault of a young woman, the police rounded up the usual suspects for a lineup. Suddenly, the Welsh suspect stepped forward and screamed "That's her!"

****

The only real problem holding women back is men.

****

A painting contractor was speaking with a woman about the job. In the first room she said she would like a pale blue. The contractor wrote this down and went to the window, opened it, and yelled out "GREEN SIDE UP!" In the second room she told the painter she would like it painted in a soft yellow. He wrote this on his pad, walked to the window, opened it, and yelled "GREEN SIDE UP!" The lady was somewhat curious but she said nothing. In the third room she said she would like it painted a warm rose colour. The painter wrote this down, walked to the window, opened it and yelled "GREEN SIDE UP!" The lady then asked him, "Why do you keep yelling 'green side up'?" "I'm sorry," came the reply. "But I have a crew of Essex girls laying turf across the street."

****

What do you get when you offer an Essex girl a penny for her thoughts? Change.

****

What do you see when you look into an Essex girl's eyes? The back of her head.

****

What do you get when you cross an Essex girl and a lawyer? I don't know, there are some things even an Essex girl won't do.

Mr Smith: "Roger, where was yer son-in-law when y' first saw'n?"
Mr Jones: "Right smack in t' middle of my sights."

****

A Welshman goes to a whorehouse. The Madam is out of women but, since the guy is Welsh, she thinks she can get away with a blow-up doll and he will never know the difference. Being a bit nervous because she has never tried this one before, the Madam waits outside the door. The Welshman comes out in five minutes. "How was it?" says the Madam. "I don't know," says the Welshman, "I bit her on the tit and she farted and flew out the window."

****

There was a Cornish girl who finally found a good job in the city. One night, shortly after arriving in the city she was invited to a very exclusive party. She didn't know anyone, so she was trying to find someone to talk to, when she saw an elegantly-dressed lady standing alone. She approached the lady and said, "Where'm you from?" The lady gave an indignant look and said, "Well! Where I am from, we DON'T end our sentences with a preposition. The young girl thought about it and replied, "oh, well, where'm you from, slag?"

****

What about the Essex girl who gave birth to twins? Her husband is out looking for the other man.

****

How does a Cornishman know when his girlfriend is having an orgasm? He doesn't care.

****

Why can`t Essex girls water-ski? When they get their crotch wet they think they have to lay down.

****

What do you call it when an Essex girl dyes her hair brunette? Artificial intelligence.

****

Essex girl: "Excuse me sir, what time is it?" Man: "It's 3pm." Essex girl: (with a puzzled look on her face) "You know, it's the weirdest thing, but I've been asking that question all day, and each time I get a different answer."

****

Did you hear about the Welshman who studied for five days? He was scheduled to take a urine test.

****

How do you get a Welshman out of the bath tub? Throw in a bar of soap.

****

Did you hear about the Welsh helicopter crash? The pilot got cold, so he turned off the fan.

****

Did you hear about the Welsh girl who tried to trade her menstrual cycle in for a Honda?

****

Did you hear about the Welsh kamikaze pilot? He flew more than 48 successful missions.

****

Did you know that the Welsh firing squad stands in a circle?

How do you sink a Welsh battleship? Put it in water.

****

How do you stop a Welsh army on horseback? Turn off the carousel.

****

Why did the Essex girl want to become a veterinarian? Because she loved children.

****

A Welshman saw a priest walking down the street. Noticing his collar, he stopped him and said, "excuse me, but why are you wearing your shirt backwards?" The priest laughed, "because, my son, I am a Father." The Welshman scratched his head. "But I am a father too, and I don't wear my shirt backwards." Again the priest laughed. "But I am a Father of thousands." To which the Welshman replied, "well then you should wear your shorts backwards."

****

Why wasn't Christ born in Wales? Because they couldn't find three wise men and a virgin.

Why do Essex girls have vaginas? So guys will talk to them at parties.

****

What's the most popular pick up line in Truro? "Nice tooth, midear."

****

Maggie's first pregnancy had produced triplets. With considerable pride she was telling her Essex girlfriend how this happened once in every 200,000 times. The Essex girl's eyes widened: "how did you ever find time to do any housework?"

****

A 12-year-old boy comes up to the Welshman and says, "I was looking in your bedroom window last night and I saw your wife giving you a blow job. Ha ha!" The Welshman answers, "the joke's on you, Ivor. I wasn't even home last night."

****

Nappies and government ministers need to be changed frequently, and for much the same reason.

****

Three men are travelling in the Amazon, a German, an Englishman, and a Welshman, and they get captured by some Amazons. The head of the tribe says to the German, "what do you want on your back for your whipping?" The German responds, "I will take oil." So they put oil on his back, and a large Amazon whips him ten times. When he is finished the German has these huge welts on his back, and he can hardly move. The Amazons haul the German away, and say to the Welshman, "what do you want on your back?" "I will take nothing," says the Welshman, and he stands there straight and takes his ten lashings without a single flinch. "What will you take on your back?" the Amazons ask the Englishman. He responds, "I'll take the Welshman."

****

An Englishman is walking down the street when he sees a Welshman with a very long pole and a yardstick. He's standing the pole on its end and trying to reach the top of it with his yardstick. Seeing the Welshman's ignorance, the Englishman wrenches the pole out of his hand, lays it on the sidewalk, measures it with the yardstick, and says, "there, ten feet long." The Welshman grabs the yardstick and shouts, "you idiot! I don't care how long it is, I want to know how high it is."

****

They put one man on the moon. Why can't they put them all there?

Men call us birds, is that because of all the worms we pick up?

****

Heard about the Welsh hockey team? They all drowned in spring training.

****

Why did the Essex girl take two hits of acid? She wanted to go on a round trip.

****

Why did the Essex girl stare at orange juice for two hours? Because it said 'concentrate'.

****

How does an Essex girl spell farm? E-I-E-I-O.

****

Why did the Essex girl snort Nutra-Sweet? She thought it was diet coke.

What does an Essex girl say after multiple orgasms? Way to go, team!

****

Who wears a dirty white robe and rides a sheep? Lawrence of Wales.

****

Why did the Essex girl put her finger over the nail when she was hammering? The noise gave her a headache.

****

What's delaying the Welsh space program? Development of a working match.

****

Why are Essex girls like pianos? When they aren't upright, they're grand.

****

How do you describe the perfect Essex girl? Three feet tall, no teeth, and a flat head to rest your beer on.

How does an Essex girl part her hair? By doing the splits.

****

A Welshman is hired to paint the lines on the road. On the first day he paints ten miles, and his employers are amazed. But, the second day he painted just five, and on only the third day, he painted only a mile of the road. Disappointed, his boss asks what the problem was. The Welshman replies, "well sir, every day I have to walk farther and farther to get back to the paint bucket."

****

How do you get a one-armed Essex girl out of a tree? Wave to her.

****

How do you get a one-armed Welshman out of a tree? Wave to him.

****

In Cornwall in the good old days, men were "real" men, women were "real" women, and small furry animals were "real" small furry animals. You knew where you stood. If you didn't, you planted a flag in the ground and claimed the place for King and Country, and everyone else knew where you stood. Nowadays, Cornishmen wear long hair and Cornishwomen wear trousers. People have sex with other people regardless of gender or species. Men are "real" women, women are "real" men, and small furry animals are real afraid.

****

Boys will be boys but one day all girls will be women.

****

What's an Essex girl's idea of safe sex? Locking the car door.

****

Wales sent its top team of scientists to attend the international science convention, where all the countries of the world gathered to compare their scientific achievements and plans. The scientists listened to the United States describe how they were another step closer to a cure for cancer, how the Russians were preparing a space ship to go to Saturn, and how Germany was inventing a car that runs on water. Soon, it was the Welsh scientists' turn to speak. "Well, we are preparing a space ship to fly to the sun." This, of course was met with much ridicule. They were asked how they planned to deal with the sun's extreme heat. "Simple, we're going at night."

Did you hear in the news that a 747 recently crashed in a cemetery in Wales? The Welsh officials have so far retrieved 2000 bodies.

****

Did you hear about the new automatic Welsh parachutes? They open on impact.

****

The May Day parade in Moscow is the largest, most important military parade of the year. For the 1993 parade, Yeltsin and Gorbachev invited Bill Clinton to come and watch it with them. The parade commenced with a battalion of tanks, followed by a division of infantry, followed by armoured personnel carriers and mobile artillery. They had mobile ballistic missile launchers, electronic jamming vehicles, and throughout the entire time the formations were overflown by squadrons of the most advanced interceptors, fighters, and long-range tactical and strategic bombers. Clinton was suitably impressed. Then he noticed that, way back at the end of the parade, there was a disorganized, messy bunch of men in rumpled suits tagging along behind the last artillery pieces. "Who are they?" he asked. "Ah," said Yeltsin, "those are our economists." "But I thought this parade was military..." said Clinton, confused. "Mr Clinton," said Gorbachev, "have you SEEN the damage those men can do?"

Have you seen the Welsh mine detector? He puts his fingers in his ears and starts stamping the ground with his foot.

****

In Truro recently three armed men robbed a jeweller and decided to use his car for a getaway vehicle. Exiting the shop, they all piled into the car, only to discover that it had a manual gearstick, which none of the three knew how to operate... They were last seen fleeing on foot.

****

Why do Essex girls hate M&Ms? They're too hard to peel.

****

Two Welsh hunters were out looking for pheasant when they came upon the local farmer's daughter, sitting naked on a fence, sunning herself. The first hunter asked, "are you game?" She replied, "I sure am, baby." The second hunter shot her.

****

What are the three biggest lies a Cornishman tells? 1) Yes, I do really have an O-level. 2) No, she's not my cousin. 3) Honest officer, I was only trying to help the sheep over the fence.

What do you call the layer of sweat between two Cornish folk having sex? Relative humidity.

****

Did you hear about the latest Welsh invention? It's a solar-powered flashlight.

****

The trouble with some women is that they get all excited about nothing and then marry him.

****

After the PLO and Israel shook hands and said that everything was fine, Clinton invited the Israeli Prime Minister back to the Oval Office. The Prime Minister looked at Clinton's desk and noticed that he had three phones, a black one, a red one, and a white one. The Prime Minister asked, "what is the red phone for?" Clinton said, "It's a direct line to Russia. Got to keep up with Yeltsin." Then the Prime Minister asked, "what's the white one for, then?" Clinton said, "that's a direct line to God. Did you know that it's a $5,000,000 a minute phone call to him?" The Prime Minister just nodded and went on with the tour. Weeks later, Clinton took a secret trip to Israel and, while he was there, toured the Prime Minister's office. He noticed that the

Prime Minister had three phones just like his. He asked, "what's the red phone for?" The Prime minister replied, "it's a direct line to Russia." Clinton nodded and then asked, "what's the white one for?" The Prime Minister replied, "it's a direct line to God." Clinton said, "how can a poor country like yours afford such an expensive phone call?" The Prime Minister said, "oh, well, from here it's local rate..."

****

A young Essex woman is asked out on a date and accepts. The boy picks her up and they go to a nearby carnival in town. They ride a few rides, play a few games, and seem to be generally hitting it off well. During a sort of romantic lull, however, the boy says, "What do you want to do now?" "I want a weigh," she says. Well, okay, thinks the boy. They walk over to the fortune scales, and weigh her. They play a few more games and stop for food. "What do you want to do now?" asks the boy again. "I want a weigh," she says. Hmmm, a little odd but I'll put up with it, thinks the boy. Again they get her weight and fortune. After yet another few games and an exquisite fireworks show, the boy repeats, "what do you want to do now?" "I want a weigh," she says. Damn, thinks the boy, she's just too weird for me. They get her weight and fortune, and the boy drives her home. As she walks into the house, her sister asks, "how'd your date go?" "Wousy," says the girl.

****

Two Welsh hunters were driving in the US, bear hunting. They came upon a fork in the road where a sign read "BEAR LEFT". They went home.

****

A Welshman wanted to learn how to sky dive. He got an instructor and started lessons. The instructor told the Welshman to jump out of the plane and pull his rip cord. The instructor then explained that he himself would jump out right behind him so that they would go down together. The Welshman understood and was ready. The time came for the Welshman to jump and the instructor reminded the man that he would be right behind him. The Welshman jumped from the plane and, after being in the air for a few seconds, pulled the rip cord. The instructor followed by jumping from the plane but when he pulled his rip cord the parachute did not open. The instructor, frantically trying to get his parachute open, darted past the Welshman. The Welshman seeing this yelled, as he undid the straps to his parachute, "so you wanna race, eh?"

****

Every man has it in his power to make one woman happy... by remaining a bachelor.

****

Why did the Welshman sell his water skis? He couldn't find a lake with a hill in it.

****

Why did the Essex girl have blisters on her lips? From trying to blow out light bulbs.

****

What is the definition of gross ignorance? 144 Essex girls.

****

A Welshman, an Englishman, and a Frenchman are running away from the German soldiers when they come up to a forest and they decide to hide by each climbing a tree. When the Germans arrive, they go to the first tree where the English guy is, and shout, "we know you're up there; come down." The English guy, thinking fast, says, "twit, twit, twit..." The Germans, thinking that it's a bird, move on to the next tree where the French guy is and once again shout, "we know you're up there; come down." The French guy, thinking fast, says, "woo, woo, woo..." The Germans, thinking that it's an owl, move on to the next tree where the Welsh guy is and once again shout, "we know you're up there; come down." The Welsh guy thinks for a while and then says, "moo, moo, moo..."

Why do Welsh police cars have stripes on the side? So the cops can find the handles.

****

What's the difference between a good old boy and a Cornishman? The good old boy raises sheep. The Cornishman gets emotionally involved.

****

Mr Smith: "What'm yer son goin' t' be when he graduates, midear?"
Mr Jones: "An old man, I fancy."

****

Did you hear about the gay Welshman? He slept with women.

****

Why do blondes have more fun? Because they are easier to find in the dark.

****

What is the Essex girl's favourite battery? Ever-ready.

What is 68 to an Essex girl? Where she goes down on you and you owe her one.

****

What's the difference between an Essex girl and an ice cream cone? Ice cream cones don't lick back.

****

What's the difference between an Essex girl and a light bulb? The light bulb is smarter, but the Essex girl is easier to turn on.

****

What can save a dying Essex girl? Hair transplants.

What's the difference between an Essex girl and a brick? When you lay a brick it doesn't follow you around for two weeks whining.

****

What's the first thing an Essex girl does in the morning? She introduces herself.

Did you hear about the Essex couple who were found frozen to death in their car at a drive-in cinema? They went to see "Closed for the Winter".

****

Did you hear about the Essex girl who robbed a bank? She tied up the safe and blew the guard.

****

Did you hear about the Essex girl with a Masters degree in Psychology? She'll blow your mind, too.

****

Did you here about the Essex girl who shot an arrow into the air? She missed.

****

What did the really dumb Essex girl say when someone blew in her bra? Thanks for the refill.

****

What is the difference between Essex girls and traffic signs? Some traffic signs say stop.

****

What do UFOs and smart Essex girls have in common? You keep hearing about them, but never see any.

****

How do you keep an Essex girl busy all day? Put her in a round room and tell her to sit in the corner.

****

What do you give the Essex girl that has everything? Penicillin.

****

How do you measure an Essex girl's intelligence? Stick a tyre-pressure gauge in her ear.

****

What do you call an Essex girl with a bag of sugar on her head? Sweet Fuck All...

What do you call an Essex girl golfer with an IQ of 125? A foursome.

****

How do you know an Essex girl has just lost her virginity? Her crayons are still sticky.

****

How do you get an Essex girl to marry you? Tell her she's pregnant.

****

What do you call an Essex girl's mother-in-law? An air bag.

****

How do you describe an Essex girl, surrounded by a bunch of drooling idiots? Flattered.

****

How do you confuse an Essex girl? You don't. They're born that way.

****

What do you call four Essex girls lying on the ground? An air mattress.

****

What is the Essex girl doing when she holds her hands tightly over her ears? Trying to hold on to a thought.

****

A Cornishman is visiting his cousin's farm, and the farmer shows him round the chicken sheds, the pig pens, the paddocks and so on. Finally he points to a tree about 30 feet away and tells the first guy: "under that tree is where I first had sex." Then he points to another tree and says: "... and that's where her mother stood and watched us." The first guy gasps and asks: "what did she say?" His cousin grins, and replies: "baaa."

****

Why did the Welsh couple decide to have only four children? They'd read in the newspaper that one out of every five babies born in the world today is Chinese.

****

A Welshman was walking down the street, carrying a brown paper bag. He ran into one of his friends, who asked, "hey! What do you have in the bag?" The man told his friend that he had some fish in the bag. His friend said, "well, I'll make you a bet. If I can guess how many fish you have in the bag, you'll have to give me one." The man says, "I'll tell you what. If you tell me how many fish I have in this bag, I'll give you both of them."

****

What do you call an Essex girl between two brunettes? A mental block.

****

This Welshman came home one day from work, hung up his coat, took off his hat and walked into his bedroom shouting "I'm home, darling." What should he see but his best friend in bed with his wife. Infuriated, he rushed to the cupboard, pulled out his gun and put it to his head. His wife started laughing. "Don't laugh," he screamed, "you're next."

****

A travelling salesman has an audience with the new Pope David and, not quite knowing what to say, tries to break the ice with a joke...

"Have you heard the one about the two Welsh priests, Holy Father?" "But I am Welsh, my son." There followed a pregnant pause while the salesman thought quickly ... "That's okay, Holy Father, I'll tell it to you slowly."

****

Did you hear about the Cornishman who passed away and left his entire estate in trust for his widow? She can't touch it till she's 14...

****

Why are Essex girls like cornflakes? Because they're simple, easy and they taste good.

****

A Welshman was suffering from constipation, so his doctor prescribed suppositories. A week later the man complained to the doctor that they didn't produce the desired results. "Have you been taking them regularly?" the doctor asked. "What do you think I've been doing," the man said, "shoving them up my ass?"

****

A Welshman went to a carpenter and said: "can you build me a box that is 2 inches high, 2 inches wide, and 50 feet long?" "Hmm," mused the carpenter, "it could be done, I suppose, but what would you want a box like that for?" "Well, you see," said the Welshman, "my neighbour moved away and forgot his garden hose."

****

An Essex girl and a brunette were discussing their boyfriends. Brunette: "Last night I had three orgasms in a row." Essex girl: "That's nothing; last night I had over a hundred." Brunette: "My god! I had no idea he was that good." Essex girl: (looking shocked) "Oh, you mean with one guy."

****

An Essex girl and her boyfriend were sharing a bath. The Essex girl said to her boyfriend: "Is it true that if you pull your finger out, I'll sink?"

****

Where do Cornishmen meet girls? At family barbecues.

****

Two Cornishmen were standing around on a sheep farm, during the coldest winter they'd had in years. Bill turned to Roger and confessed that he really couldn't wait until it was time to shear the flocks. The other nodded, rubbing his hands together in anticipation. "We'm be having a top time selling t' wool, and spending t' money on beer and women, eh?" "No, that bain't it," said Bill, "I'm just carn't wait t' see'm naked."

****

An Englishman, a Frenchman and a Welshman are captured and thrown into prison. However, the guard is rather kind towards them, and says, "I am going to lock you away for five years, but I'll let you have anything you want now before I lock you away." The Englishman says: "I'll have five years' supply of beer." His wish is granted, and they lock him away with his beer. The Frenchman says: "I'll have five years' supply of brandy." His wish is granted, and they lock him away with his brandy. The Welshman says: "I'll have five years' supply of cigarettes." His wish is granted, and they lock him away with his cigarettes. Five years later the prisoners are released. First, they release the Englishman, who staggers out totally drunk. Then, they release the Frenchman, who also rolls out rather inebriated. Then, they release the Welshman, who comes out and says: "has anyone got a light?"

****

Theme Nights

9

Jokes about Guitarists, Students and Nuns

What should you do if you run over a guitar? Reverse.

****

Mother Superior: "Sister Maria, if you were walking through town at night, and were accosted by a man with bad intentions, what would you do?" Sister Maria: "I would lift my habit, Mother Superior." Mother Superior (shocked): "and what would you do next?" Sister Maria "I would tell him to drop his trousers." Mother Superior: (even more shocked) "and what then?" Sister Maria: "I would run away. I can run much faster with my habit up than he can with his trousers down."

****

What do you get when you throw a guitar and an accordion off the Empire State Building? Applause.

****

Never let your schooling interfere with your education.

****

One can pity the father with three kids at university. He tells his wife that they are getting poorer by degrees.

College: the fountains of knowledge where everyone goes to drink.

****

A nun and a priest were travelling across the desert and realized halfway across that the camel they were using for transportation was about to die. They set up a make-shift camp, hoping that someone would come to their rescue, but to no avail. Soon the camel died. After several days of not being rescued, they agreed that they were not going to be rescued. They prayed a lot (of course), and they discussed their predicament in great depth. Finally the priest said to the nun, "you know, Sister, I am about to die, and there's always been one thing I've wanted here on Earth – to see a woman naked. Would you mind taking off your clothes so I can look at you?" The nun thought about his request for several seconds and then agreed to take off her clothes. As she was doing so, she remarked, "well, Father, now that I think about it, I've never seen a man naked, either. Would you mind taking off your clothes, too?" With a little hesitation, the priest also stripped. Suddenly the nun exclaimed, "Father! What is that little thing hanging between your legs?" The priest patiently answered, "that, my child, is a gift from God. If I put it in you, it creates a new life." "Well," responded the nun, "forget about me. Stick it in the camel."

****

It is Friday, and four nuns go to the priest at the local catholic church to ask for the weekend off. They argue for a few minutes but finally the priest agrees to let them leave the convent for the weekend. "However," he says, "as soon as you get back on Monday morning I want you to confess to me what you have done over the weekend." The four nuns agree, and run off. Monday comes, and the four nuns return. The first nun goes to the priest and says: "forgive me, Father, for I have sinned." The priest asks: "what did you do, Sister?" She replies: "I watched an X-rated movie." The priest looks up at heaven for a few seconds, then replies: "you are forgiven. Go and drink the holy water." The first nun leaves, and the fourth nun begins to chuckle quietly under her breath. The second nun then goes up to the priest and says: "forgive me , Father, for I have sinned." The priest replies: "okay, what happened?" She says: "I was driving my brother's car down the street in front of his house and I hit a neighbour's dog and killed it." The priest looks up to heaven for half a minute, then says: "you are forgiven. Go and drink the holy water." The second nun goes out. By this time, the fourth nun is laughing quite audibly. Then the third nun walks to the priest and says: "forgive me, Father, for I have sinned." The priest asks: "out with it. What did you do?" She says: "last night, I ran naked up and down Main Street." The priest looks up at heaven for a full five minutes before responding: "God forgives you. Go and drink the holy water." She leaves. The fourth nun falls on the floor, laughing so hard tears run down her cheeks. The priest asks her: "okay. What did you do that was so funny?" The fourth nun replies: "I pissed in the holy water..."

Guitar pickers: we tune because we care...

****

What's the best or fastest way to tune a guitar? With wire-cutters.

****

One day, a very attractive undergraduate visited the professor's office. She pulled the chair closer to the professor, smiled at him shyly, bumped his knee "accidentally", and so on. Finally, the undergraduate said: "professor, I really need to pass your course. It is extremely important to me. It is so important that I'll do anything you suggest." The professor, somewhat taken aback by this attention, replied: "anything?" To which the undergraduate cooed: "yes, anything you say." After some brief reflection, the professor asked: "what are you doing tomorrow afternoon at 3pm?" The student lied: "oh, nothing at all, sir. I can be free then." The professor then advised: "excellent! Professor Palmer is holding a help session for his students. Why don't you attend that."

****

No matter how much you tune it, it will still sound like a guitar!

****

Why don't guitar pickers like to go to the beach? Because cats keep trying to bury them.

****

Why don't guitar players get to take breaks between sets? It takes them too long to retune.

****

When professors want your opinion, they'll give it to you.

****

How can you tell if there's a guitar player at your door? They can't find the key, the knocking speeds up, and they don't know when to come in.

****

When do guitar songs sound the best? When they're over.

****

What do you say to the guitar player wearing a three piece suit? "Will the defendant please rise."

How can you tell if the stage is level? If the guitar player drools out of both sides of his mouth.

****

There are two nuns in a bath. The first one says: "Where's the soap." The second one replies: "yes it does, doesn't it."

****

Student: "What's your opinion on the paper I submitted last week?" Professor: "It's absolute drivel." Student: "I know, but let's hear it anyway."

****

While visiting a country school, the chairman of the Board Of Education became provoked at the noise the unruly students were making in the next room. Angrily, he opened the door and grabbed one of the taller boys who seemed to be doing most of the talking. He dragged the boy into the next room and stood him in the corner. A few minutes later, a small boy stuck his head in the room and pleaded, "please, sir, may we have our teacher back?"

****

Sister Catherine is asking all the catholic school children in fourth grade what they want to be when they grow up. Little Sheila says: "when I grow up, I want to be a prostitute!" Sister Catherine's eyes grow wide and she barks: "what in the name of God did you say?" "A prostitute," Sheila repeats. Sister Catherine breathes a sight of relief and says: "thank God! I thought you said a Protestant."

****

There was a story around Oxford that the final exam on a maths degree always read: "Make up an appropriate final exam for this course and answer it. You will be graded on both parts." Then one year, a student answered as follows: "the exam question is: 'make up an appropriate final exam for this course and answer it. You will be graded on both parts.' The answer is: 'make up an appropriate final exam for this course and answer it. You will be graded on both parts.'" His reasoning was that since that was the best exam the professor could write, it certainly ought to be good enough for a student. He got an A. The professor specifically prohibited that answer from then on.

****

A professor is one who talks in someone else's sleep.

****

Why did the Boy Scout take up the guitar? They make good paddles.

****

What is the definition of something suspicious? A nun doing press-ups in a cucumber field.

****

There were these three catering students driving along an old country road one day when they saw a farm. So they pulled in, and knocked on the farmer's door. The farmer answered the door and the three students introduced themselves and said: "we were just passing by and saw your field of buttercups and were wondering if we could go and get a bucket full of butter?" The old farmer scratched his head and said: "you boys ain't gonna get no butter from buttercups but you're more than welcome to try." About an hour later, the three came back, thanked the farmer, and drove off with their bucket full of butter. The farmer once again scratched and shook his head, mumbled under his breath and went on about his business. About three months later, the same three students came up to the farm, knocked on the door, and asked the farmer if he remembered them. He chuckled and asked what he could do for them this time? One of them said: "we were just driving by and happened to see you now have a field of milkweed and we were wondering if we could go out and get a bucket of milk?" Once again, the old farmer chuckled, shook his head, scratched it and sarcastically said: "you boys go on out there and get your milk from my milkweeds." Once again, about an hour later, the three came back with their bucket overflowing with fresh milk and drove off. This time, the farmer was really confused, but just a little less sceptical. It was about three or four months later when the three agricultural students came back and again knocked on the farmer's door, this time saying that they were driving by and saw the field full of pussywillows. This time the farmer went with them.

****

If you took all the students that fell asleep in class and laid them end to end, they'd be a lot more comfortable.

****

Guitars are to music as Spam is to food...

****

What's the difference between a skunk run over on the road and a guitar player run over on the road? You see skid marks in front of the skunk.

****

Did you hear about the skeleton they just found in an old building at Roehampton College? It was the 1938 hide and seek champion.

****

At a convention of biological scientists one researcher remarks to another: "did you know that in our lab we have switched from mice to guitar players for our experiments?" "Really?" the other replies, "why did you switch?" "Well, for several reasons. We found that guitar players are far more plentiful; the lab assistants don't get so attached to them; the animal rights activists leave us alone; and there are some things even a rat won't do... However, sometimes it is very hard to extrapolate our test results to human beings."

****

The seven dwarfs are in Rome and they go on a tour of the city. After a while they go to the Vatican and Grumpy gets to meet the Pope privately. Grumpy, for once, seems to have a lot to say; he keeps asking the pontiff questions about the church, and in particular, nuns. "Your Holiness, do you have any really short nuns?" "No, my son, all our nuns are at least 5 feet tall." "Are you sure? I mean, you wouldn't have any nuns that are, say, about my height? Maybe a little shorter?" "I'm afraid not. Why do you ask?" "No reason." Pause. "Positive? Nobody in a habit that's about 3 feet tall, 2 feet tall?" "I'm sure." "Okay." Grumpy looks dejected at this news, and the Pope wonders why. So he listens to the dwarves as they leave the building. "What'd he say? What'd he say?" chant the other six. Grumpy says: "he said they don't have any." And the other six start chanting: "Grumpy fucked a penguin! Grumpy fucked a penguin! Grumpy fucked a penguin!"....

****

A catering student decides to raise chickens, so he goes to the pet shop and buys some baby chicks. He takes the chicks home, and plants them with their heads sticking up. He waters them, but they die. He goes back to the shop and tells the proprietor that he bought defective chicks, and gets another set. This time he plants them with their heads sticking down. He waters them, but they die. Finally he sends a letter to his old college, describing the problem and asking for advice. They send a letter back asking for a soil sample.

****

Why do they let guitar players play in pizza parlours? Because pizza is the only food that you can taste over the noise.

****

What's worse than a guitar player? Two guitar players. What's worse than two guitar players? Nothing.

What's the best thing to play on a guitar? A flame-thrower.

****

What is the definition of perfect pitch? Throwing a guitar into a toilet without hitting the seat.

****

Why do so many fishermen own guitars? They make great anchors!

****

Did you hear that they outlawed "the wave" at Loughborough University? Two poor catering students drowned at a game last year.

****

I used to play guitar on TV but my Mum told me to get off before I broke it.

****

Guitar players never get out of line, just out of tune...

****

A philosophy professor stands at the front of the classroom with the following final exam question written on the blackboard: "How do you plan to make a living with a philosophy degree?"

****

How do you get a nun pregnant? Dress her up as an altar boy.

****

What do you call a nun with a sex change operation? A trans-sister.

****

What do you call a nun who walks in her sleep? A roaming catholic.

****

I recently had surgery on my hand, and asked the doctor if, after surgery, I would be able to play the guitar. He said, "I'm doing surgery on your hand, not giving you a lobotomy."

****

Guitar players play requests by multiple-choice not fill-in-the-blank.

Guitar players spend half their lives tuning and the other half playing out of tune.

****

How many catering students does it take to make chocolate chip cookies? Three: one to mix the batter and two to squeeze the rabbit.

****

How many catering students does it take to eat a hedgehog? Three: one to do the eating, and two to watch for cars.

****

A priest asks a nun if he can walk her back to the convent. She says, "just this once." Upon arriving, he asks if he can kiss her. She replies, "well, alright, as long as you don't get into the habit."

****

Did you hear that they've isolated the gene for guitar playing? It's the first step to a cure!

****

What is the definition of innocence? A nun working in a condom factory thinking she's making sleeping bags for mice.

****

"If there are any idiots in the room, will they please stand up," said the sarcastic lecturer. After a long silence, one freshman rose to his feet. "Now then mister, why do you consider yourself an idiot?" enquired the lecturer with a sneer. "Well, actually I don't," said the student, "but I hate to see you standing up there all by yourself."

****

Ice is no longer available in the drinks at the cafeterias at Aston University. The student who knew the recipe graduated.

****

Guitar player: "when I die, I want to leave the world a better place."
Piano player: "don't worry, you will."

****

Two ex-catering students decide to have a reunion. One decides to visit the other one living in a big town. The visiting student gets lost and calls his friend: "hey buddy, I am coming over but I am lost and have no idea where I am." His friend replies: "it's okay, just look at the street intersection, there will be two signs, read them to me." The lost one looks over and then says: "okay, okay, I see them, one says Walk, the other one says Do not walk." "Oh good, you are right down the street. I'll be over to pick you up."

****

Why do ghouls and demons hang out together? Because demons are a ghoul's best friend!

****

Listener: "Can you read music?" Guitar player: "Not enough to hurt my playing."

****

How can you get a guitar player's eyes to sparkle? Shine a light in her ears...

****

What's the difference between a guitar player and a puppy? If you ignore a puppy long enough it will stop whining...

What's the difference between a guitar player and a savings bond? A savings bond eventually matures and earns money.

****

What's the difference between a guitar and a lawnmower? Your wife gets upset when the neighbours borrow the lawnmower and don't return it.

****

How is lightning like a guitar player's fingers? Neither one strikes in the same place twice.

****

What is the difference between grapes and a guitar? You take off your shoes to stomp on grapes.

****

Striking teachers today rejected the government's latest pay offer saying that it was blatantly copied from a previous offer, contained too many erasures and misspellings, and was handed in late.

****

What do you call a good musician at a guitar contest? A visitor.

****

What did the guitar player get on his IQ test? Spittle

****

Three college friends, one each from the Universities of Oxford, Cambridge, and Loughborough, decided to pool their funds and go to the Olympics in Barcelona. The airfare and hotel rates ate up most of their money so they didn't have enough to get into the stadium to see the events. So they stood around the gate watching all the other people get in and then noticed that some people didn't have to pay. Whenever an athlete passed the guard with his (or her) equipment, the guard would simply nod and let them through. So the three visitors quickly trotted off to a nearby hardware shop and came back to try to get in. The Oxford student walked up to the guard and gestured at the long pole he carried. "Pole vaulting," he said, and the guard waved him through. The Cambridge student, having rigged up a ball to a length of chain, approached the guard next and showed off his wares. "Hammer throwing," he said, and the guard shrugged and waved him through. The catering student from Loughborough came last, with a roll of chain link on his shoulder. "Fencing."

****

It was a busy day for the electric chair. Three men were up for their death sentences. The first man was a political scientist from Oxford. He was strapped into the chair and asked if he had any final comments. He replied, "I had a promising career in politics until...I was framed, I tell you, framed!" His tirade was interrupted by the flick of the switch, but nothing happened. As was the custom at this particular prison, the Oxford man was taken from the chair and allowed to live after the failed execution attempt. The second man was a computer scientist from Cambridge. His final words were, "I had a promising career in computing, but I didn't think that tampering with the national air traffic control system would crash that many planes..." Again, the electrical switch was flipped and again nothing happened. The man was released from the chair and allowed to live. The third man was an electrical engineer, named Kev, from Roehampton College. Kev was strapped into the chair and asked if he had any final words. He says, "I had a promising career as an electrical engineer, but, wait a moment...., if you cross that red wire over there with that blue wire, this thing will work."

****

A professor was grading the essay finals he had just given his class and opened the exam book of a failing student to reveal blank pages and a £100 note. The only thing written in the book was "£100 = 100% – I get an A." A month later, the student approached the professor. "I don't understand," he said, "I failed the course.

Didn't you read my final?" The professor handed the student the exam book. The student opened it to reveal £50 and the phrase "£50 = 50% – you fail!"

****

How can you tell the difference between guitar songs? By their names.

****

The graduate with a science degree asks, "Why does it work?" The graduate with an engineering degree asks, "How does it work?" The graduate with a management degree asks, "How much will it cost?" The graduate with an arts degree asks, "Do you want fries with that?"

****

A student who changes the course of history is probably taking an exam.

****

How can you tell which person is the catering student on a drilling rig? He's the one throwing bread to the helicopters.

Did you hear about the catering student who was tap dancing? He broke his ankle when he fell into the sink.

****

What do guitar players and bottles of beer have in common? They're both empty from the neck up.

****

Where do guitar players play best? In traffic.

****

Why don't guitar players get any mail? Because they can't read notes.

****

Why don't catering students eat barbecue beans? Because they keep falling through the holes in the grill.

****

There is a costume party at a mental hospital. The theme of the party is war. The first person comes up on to the stage and says, "I'm an atomic bomb." He gets his applause and steps down. The second person comes up and says, "I'm a hydrogen bomb." Again, there's applause and he steps down. And then a naked little man comes up to the stage and says, "I'm dynamite." Everybody runs away hysterically. When one of them is asked why, he says, "didn't you see how small his fuse was?"

****

You're lost in the desert and you see Bugs Bunny, a cactus, and a good guitar player. Who do you ask for directions? You might as well try the cactus, the other two are figments of your imagination.

****

You're driving down the street and you see an accordion and a guitar – which one do you hit first? The accordion: business before pleasure.

****

Two nuns are walking down an alley at night. Two guys jump out and start raping them. The first nun looks to heaven and says, "forgive them Father, for they know not what they're doing." The second nun looks up and says, "this one does."

****

Why do some people take an instant aversion to guitar players? It saves time.

****

Two Texas Longhorn students and a catering student were driving through the Texas countryside when their car broke down. Luckily, they were near a farmhouse. So they knocked on the door and asked the gruff old farmer if they could stay the night. The farmer agreed, but only on one bizarre condition. He told them to go out into his field, pick any fruit or vegetable they could find, then return to the farmhouse. Some time later, the two Longhorns found themselves dead and in line at the Pearly Gates. St Peter was there, listening to their tale. "Okay," said St Peter, "you went out and found some fruits and vegetables. How did you die?" "Well," continued one of the Longhorns, "my friend here returned first with a cherry. Then the farmer pointed his gun at him and commanded, 'stick that cherry up your ass, and if you laugh I'll shoot you.'" "And?" prompted St Peter. "He laughed, and the farmer shot him." "Why did you laugh?" St Peter asked the second Longhorn. "It tickled," he said. "Then it was my turn," continued the first Longhorn. "I had also brought a cherry, and the farmer pointed his gun at me and told me the same thing. I laughed and he shot me." "And why did you laugh?" St Peter asked. "I saw the catering student coming up the walkway with a watermelon."

Why do bluegrass guitar pickers always die with their boots on? So they won't stub their toes when they kick the bucket.

****

Did you hear the one about the man who opened a dry-cleaning business next door to the convent? He knocked on the door and asked the Mother Superior if she had any dirty habits.

****

What kind of fun does a priest have? Nun.

****

What is the difference between a terrorist and a guitar player? Terrorists have sympathizers.

****

What's the difference between a guitar and a flute? Flutes don't burn!

****

Don't tell my mum I'm a guitar player. She thinks I'm a piano player in a whorehouse.

A catering student spots a professor who is staring intently into an aquarium. The catering student asks the professor: "what are you doing?" The professor answers, "I'm attempting mental telepathy with this fish. You see, if my mind is stronger than theirs, I can control their thoughts. Why don't you try it?" The catering student, certain of his ability to successfully control the fish, stares into the tank for a few seconds. Then, all of the sudden, his eyes start bulging and his mouth makes a little "o" shape...

****

What does a sperm and a guitar player have in common? They both have one chance in about a million of becoming a human being.

****

Why is a degree like a condom? It's rolled up when you get it, it represents a lot of effort, it's worthless the next day.

****

A man goes through customs with a guitar case. The inspector nervously asks the man to set the case on the table. Sweating, the inspector uses a long stick to slowly open the case. He sighs a sigh of relief when the contents reveal a machine gun and miscellaneous explosives. "Pass! For a minute there, I thought you had a guitar..."

****

How is playing the guitar a lot like throwing a javelin blindfolded? You don't have to be very good to get people's attention.

****

How can you tell if a guitar player is well hung? If you can put two fingers between his neck and the rope...

****

What has 16 legs and three teeth? The front row of a guitar workshop.

****

A nun is driving the convent's car through some very lonely countryside. The car stops and she notices there is no petrol left. So she walks to the nearest filling station. Being a nun and a little unworldly, she forgets to take along the petrol can. The nice man at the filling station has no petrol can either, so he hands her a chamber-pot full of petrol. The nun walks back to her car and starts pouring the petrol into the tank. A bypassing car stops, and the driver looks out and says: "sister, how I would like to have as much faith as you do!"

****